CURRENCY CONV

This chart provides
converted from GB pounds, based on a
conversion rate of $1.45 to the pound

£1	$1.45
£5	$7.25
£10	$14.50
£20	$29.00
£25	$36.25
£50	$72.50
£75	$108.75
£100	$145.00
£125	$181.25
£150	$217.50
£175	$253.75
£200	$290.00
£250	$362.50
£300	$435.00
£400	$580.00
£500	$725.00
£750	$1,087.50
£1,000	$1,450.00
£2,000	$2,900.00
£5,000	$7,250.00
£7,500	$10,875.00
£10,000	$14,500.00
£20,000	$29,000.00
£30,000	$43,500.00
£40,000	$58,000.00
£50,000	$72,500.00
£100,000	$145,000.00

ANTIQUES COLLECTABLES

MARTIN MILLER

CARLTON
BOOKS

CONTENTS

ACKNOWLEDGEMENTS

GENERAL EDITOR
Martin Miller

EDITORS
Simon Blake
Marianne Blake
Abigail Zoe Martin
Peter Blake

EDITORIAL CO-ORDINATORS
Marianne Blake
Abigail Zoe Martin

PHOTOGRAPHIC/PRODUCTION
CO-ORDINATOR
Marianne Blake

PHOTOGRAPHERS
Abigail Zoe Martin
James Beam Van Etten
Anna Malni
Chris Smailes
Carmen Klammer

How to Use This Book

by MARTIN MILLER

Due to the phenomenal success of my annual *Antiques Source Book*, we are now producing a series of specialist handbooks, each concentrating on a specific area of buying and collecting antiques and collectables.

Antiques: Collectables is a full-colour collectable retail price guide. The reason that it stands out from other such price guides is that we have used retailers, rather than auction houses, as our sources of information. Many of the items in this book are for sale at the time of going to press and a number, certainly some of the more arcane, will remain so for the lifespan of the book.

A reputable and experienced dealer's assessment of the price of an antique is at least as reliable – and usually a great deal more reasoned – than a price achieved at auction, and so even when the item you wish to purchase from the book turns out to have been sold, you have a reliable guide to the price you should pay when you happen upon another.

This book is designed for maximum visual interest and appeal. It can be treated as a 'through read' as well as a tool for dipping in and out of. The Contents and Index will tell you in which area to find anything which you are specifically seeking.

Should you happen upon something that you wish to buy, simply note the dealer reference to the bottom right of the entry and look up the dealer's full name and details in the Directory of Dealers section towards the back of the book. You can telephone, fax and often visit the dealer's website. All the dealers who have helped us with the book will be happy to assist you and, if the piece you wish to buy has already been sold, they will almost certainly be able to help you find another. Should you wish to sell an item, the relevant section and dealer reference will again be of help, but do not expect to be offered the same price at which the dealer is selling. We all have to make a living!

Good luck and happy hunting!

Introduction

The important rule for the collector of 'collectables' is to take care of the ephemera of today — they may be the antiques of tomorrow.

The way in which antiques are viewed and valued is constantly changing. The distinction, for instance, between 'antique', 'collectable' and 'second-hand' has become very fuzzy in recent years. Curiously, in this disposable age – or perhaps because so much is disposable – the artefacts of today are valued much more by modern collectors than their equivalents were by previous generations, who generally considered that anything owned by their parents was, prima facie, not worth having.

It's an old but true saying that what one throws away today is the collectable of tomorrow. From the soap packet to the mobile phone, all have their place in the collector's market. But watch out for the fads that hit the market with a splash and are just as soon forgotten, such as the Yo-Yo.

The most collectable items are those which are in some ways ground-breaking or revolutionary at the time: for example, radios, TVs or telephones. It is also worth collecting items which are gradually becoming obsolete in the new digital age, for instance records or tapes. Self-winding watches are also a good example of this as very few are currently being made and so their value is rising. It is not too difficult to spot the collectables of the future using this as a criterion – what about the first truly mobile phones, or lap-top computers?

The best advice for building a collection is to start with something you have a great personal interest in; this could range from the everyday to the extremely expensive piece. The collector's market is very unpredictable but can be extremely rewarding if you are lucky enough to have chosen that forgotten item that defines the period in which it was made.

The great advantages with collectables is that they do not need to be especially old and they do not need to cost a great deal of money. Take almost any disposable item commonly in use at the moment, and you can be certain that someone is building a collection of it and that, in a few years, it will be much in demand.

Start gathering the antiques of tomorrow today!

Advertising & Packaging

Shop Sign ▼
• *1940s*
A wrought iron shop sign, with
scrolled decoration surrounding
a clover leaf emblem with the
hand-painted letters "Sunshine
Bakery". In original condition.
• *102cm x 65cm*
• £220   • Old School

Dresden Figurine ▼
• *1910*
A Dresden porcelain group of
figures advertising Yardley
perfumes and soaps.
• *height 17cm*
• £350   • Huxtable's

Packet of Condoms ▲
• *1950s*
An assortment of 1950s condoms.
• *16cm x 5cm/packet*
• £10   • Huxtable's

Manufacturer's Sign ▶
• *1930s*
A sign cut from hardwood of the
figure of John Bull, advertising
John Bull Tyres.
• *height 65cm*
• £120   • Huxtable's

Ink Bottle ▼
• *1930s*
A bottle of blue black Swan ink.
• *height 8cm*
• £6   • Huxtable's

Boat Biscuit Box ◄
- *circa 1935*

A French biscuit box in the shape of the ill-fated liner, *Normandie*.
- *length 62cm*
- £350   • Huxtable's

Guinness Print ▼
- *circa 1950*

Showing a pint glass and smiling face with famous slogan: "Guinness Is Good For You".
- *78cm x 50cm*
- £14   • Magpies

Queen of Hearts Box ▼
- *circa 1920*

A sweet box from *Alice in Wonderland* in the shape of Tenniel's Queen of Hearts.
- *height 20cm*
- £75   • Huxtable's

Salt Cellar ▲
- *circa 1950*

A Sifta glass salt cellar with a bakelite top.
- *height 9cm*
- £4.50   • Magpies

Cocoa Tin ▼
- *circa 1920*

A Dutch cocoa tin from Bendorp's Cocoa, Amsterdam.
- *height 9cm*
- £20   • Huxtable's

Cigarette Sign ➤
- *circa 1920*

A Craven "A" advertising sign in blue, white and red, including one of advertising's great lies.
- *height 92cm*
- £28   • Magpies

Wills's Star Cigarettes ➤
- *circa 1920*

An enamelled point-of-sale sign in brown and orange.
- *height 28cm*
- £42   • Magpies

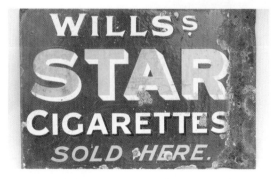

Lux Soap Flakes ▲
- *circa 1960*
An unopened box of Lever Brothers' Lux soap flakes.
- *height 28cm*
- £10   • Huxtable's

McVitie Biscuit Box ▲
- *circa 1910*
A "Billie Bird" biscuit box by McVitie.
- *height 32cm*
- £120   • Huxtable's

Toothpaste Lid ▼
- *circa 1900*
A Woods Areca Nut toothpaste lid by W. Woods, Plymouth.
- £20   • Magpies

Biscuit Tin ▼
- *circa 1910*
A biscuit tin in the shape of a book, made by Hoffman Suisse.
- *height 36cm*
- £90   • Huxtable's

Talcum Powder ▶
- *circa 1950*
A "Jolly Baby" talcum powder container, with voluptuous cover.
- *height 15cm*
- £40   • Huxtable's

Horlicks Mixer ▲
- *circa 1950*
A Horlicks promotional glass jug with a metal mixer.
- *height 15cm*
- £10   • Magpies

Battery Advertisement ◀
- *circa 1960*
An Oldham Batteries metal advertising sign, incorporating the "I told 'em – Oldham" slogan.
- *height 37cm*
- £28   • Magpies

Bottle of Broseden ▲
- *1930s*

A bottle of "Broseden" made in Germany. A drink used to calm the troops during lonely times.
- *height 9cm*
- £5   • Huxtable's

Bournvita Mug ▲
- *1950s*

A white Bournvita mug in the shape of a face with a blue nightcap and a red pom-pom. With large handle.
- *height 14cm*
- £40   • Huxtable's

Toffee Tin ▲
- *20th century*

A Macintosh's toffee tin commemorating the marriage of George VI to Elizabeth Bowes-Lyon.
- *diameter 14cm*
- £20   • Huxtable's

Brilliantine ◄
- *1930s*

A glass bottle of "Saturday Night Lotion", men's hair styling gloss.
- *height 13cm*
- £12   • Huxtable's

Carton of Cigarettes ▲
- *1960s*

A carton of Senior Service cigarettes. In original white paper wrapping with navy blue lettering, unopened.
- *13cm x 5cm*
- £40   • Huxtable's

Nib Boxes ◄
- *1920s*

An assortment of unopened nib boxes.
- *width 7cm*
- £7   • Huxtable's

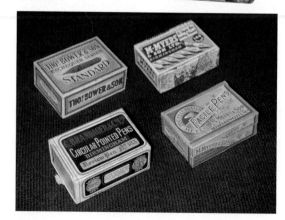

Guinness Trays >
- *circa 1950*

A metal drinks tray with a toucan holding the advertisement for Guinness.
- *diameter 16cm*
- £50 • Huxtable's

Dog Food Sign ▲
- **1950**

A Spratt's wooden sign advertising dog food with the picture of a Highland terrier in the form of the word "Spratts".
- *50cm x 80cm*
- £100 • Huxtable's

Guinness Toucan ▼
- **1955**

A toucan with a glass of Guinness on a stand advertising the beer with the slogan –
"My goodness – my Guinness".
- *height 7cm*
- £250 • Huxtable's

Lollipop Man ▲
- **1960s**

A porcelain figure of a Robertson's Golly Lollipop Man.
- *height 12cm*
- £12 • Huxtable's

Mustard Tins ▲
- *1930s*

An assortment of Coleman's mustard tins. Decorated with red writing and the Union Jack on a yellow background.
- *height 12cm*
- £7 • Huxtable's

Guinness Tray ▲
- *circa 1950*

Circular tray advertising Guinness.
- £50 • Huxtable's

Motoring Key Rings ▲
- **1960s**

Assortment of motoring key rings.
- £10 • Huxtable's

Trumps Markers ◄
- *1930s*

Two trumps markers for use in card games.
- £20 • Huxtable's

Aeronautica

BOAC Sales Leaflet ◄
- *circa 1970*
Advertising standard
merchandise of the era. With
colour pictures.
- *length 20cm*
- £10
- • Cobwebs

Aero Club Badge ▼
- *circa 1920*
Brooklands club badge in pressed
steel with coloured enamels.The
club was established in the 1920s.
- *height 10cm*
- £600
- • CARS

Model Kit ▲
- *circa 1940*
"Robot Bomb" balsa-wood model
of a jet-propelled bomb used
against England by the Germans
in France during World War II.
- £10
- • Cobwebs

Aerial ABC Gazetteer ▲
- *August 1929*
Light brown in colour with black
and white print. In mint
condition.
- *22cm x 14.5cm*
- £40
- • Cobwebs

Spanish Airline Leaflet ◄
- *circa 1922*
In good condition, but with a
folding crease down the centre.
- *15.5cm x 12cm*
- £25
- • Cobwebs

Fighter Plane Model ▼
- *circa 1980*
Model of a battle-camouflaged
Tornado fighter plane. On a steel
frame with rubber feet.
- *height 10cm*
- £30
- • Cobwebs

Expert Tips

*The most enduringly collectable
aeronautical artefacts tend still
to be those of World War II
and, most particularly, those
relating to the Battle of
Britain, 1940.*

Qantas Empire Airways ►
- *circa 1930*
A Qantas flying-boat map of the
Sydney to Singapore route. Good
condition.
- *length 24.5cm, width 12cm*
- £50
- • Cobwebs

Souvenir Programme ▲
- 1930

Illustrated souvenir programme from the British Hospitals' Air Pageant, 1930. In good condition.
- *21.5cm x 14cm*
- £40 • Cobwebs

Expert Tips

Early aerospace companies were nearly as prolific in their day as dot.com companies today. The merchandising materials of these long-dead organisations often fetch a fortune.

Promotional Magazine ▶
- *circa 1917*

Whitehead aircraft company promotional magazine. In good condition with black and white and colour prints.
- *19cm x 12cm*
- £30 • Cobwebs

Airship Safety Award ▼
- *circa 1959*

An American "Aviation Safety Award" with brass engraving set in a plaque of beechwood.
- *16cm x 13cm*
- £25-30 • Cobwebs

Aerial Timetable ▶
- *1927*

"International Aerial Time Table" in good condition and in colour print, with a fascinating cover picture of unlikely flyers.
- *21.5cm x 14cm*
- £50 • Cobwebs

Aircraft Propellor ▲
- *circa 1920*

A four-bladed wooden coarse-pitched, wind-generator propellor, in mahogany with lamination and holes in the centre intact.
- *length 61cm*
- £165 • Cobwebs

Model Airplane ▼
- *circa 1940*

Chrome model, twin-engined unidentified American plane.
- *height 10cm*
- £65 • Cobwebs

Concorde Postal Cover ◀
- *circa 1978*

Commemorating the first flight from London to New York, with colour print showing an early Concorde in blue sky.
- *19cm x 11.5cm*
- £15 • Cobwebs

Bicycles

Arnold Schwin Parckard ➤
- *circa 1930*
American lady's bicycle, with pedal back brake, maroon finish, single-speed. Very good condition.
- *66cm wheel*
- £550
- Bridge Bikes

Raleigh Rocky II ➤
- *1986*
Raleigh Rocky II with fifteen Shimano gears.
- *153cm frame*
- *66cm wheel*
- £200
- G Whizz

Raleigh Roadster ▲
- *circa 1950*
Single-speed post-war bike. Good rideable condition, with Westwood rims and rod brakes.
- *66cm wheel*
- £50
- G Whizz

Expert Tips

There is no doubt that fear for the ozone layer and the increasing vilification of the motorcar has led to an upsurge in the popularity of the bicycle. They need to be in good condition and working.

Italian Legnano ▲
- *circa 1940*
Lady's cycle, single-speed, unique rod brakes running through handlebars, full chain cover.
- *66cm wheel*
- £100
- Bridge Bikes

Humber Gents ▼
- *circa 1940*
Gent's bike with enclosed chain, three-speed hub, rod brake.
- *156cm frame*
- *71cm wheel*
- £150
- Bridge Bikes

Rival of Norwich ◄
- *circa 1930*
Lady's roadster. Unusual make and very collectable.
- *155cm seat tube*
- *63cm wheel*
- £50
- G Whizz

Bottles

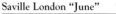

Saville London "June" ▼
- *circa 1930*
A novelty perfume bottle in the form of a sundial.
- £125   • Linda Bee

Prince Matchabello "Beloved" ▲
- *circa 1950*
Enamel crown bottle. With inner and outer box.
- £220   • Linda Bee

Silver Scent Bottle ▲
- *circa 1886*
An English, decorative silver scent bottle with scrolls and a cut-glass stopper.
- *height 5.5cm*
- £250   • John Clay

French Glass Perfume ▼
- *1860*
Mazarin blue glass perfume bottle with floral gilding and large octagonal stopper.
- *height 16cm*
- £145   • Trio

Bourjois Kobako ▲
- *circa 1925*
A fashionable oriental-style perfume bottle, designed by Bourjois of Paris, with bakelite cover and carved stand.
- £390   • Linda Bee

Schiaparelli Bottle ▲
- *circa 1938*
A Schiaparelli perfume bottle of twisted and fluted design with red finial top and beaded base.
- £180   • Linda Bee

European Perfume ▶
- *1880*
Perfume bottle of latissimo glass with engraved silver cover with glass stopper inside.
- £190   • Trio

Guerlain "L'Heure Bleue" ▼

- *circa 1940*
Made by Baccarate perfume, with
original box.
- £125   • Linda Bee

Grossmith "Old Cottage" Lavender Water ▲

- *circa 1930*
A bottle of English lavender
water of etched glass.
- £95   • Linda Bee

Nina Ricci "Coeur-Joie" ▼

- *1946*
Lalique bottle with heart-shaped
centre and floral decoration.
- £210   • Linda Bee

Conical Bottle ▼

- *circa 1866*
A mid-Victorian silver fluted
perfume bottle, of conical form,
with silver stopper.
- £210   • Trio

Bohemian Glass Bottle ▲

- *circa 1860*
Floral perfume bottle, in
Bohemian glass, with enamelling
and large cut stopper.
- £300   • Trio

Unknown Heart-Shaped Perfume Bottle ▼

- *circa 1940*
With etched glass and bakelite
base with dipper.
- £65   • Linda Bee

French Apothecary's Bottles ➤

- *19th century*
Collection of nine apothecary's
bottles including stoppers.
- £655 set   • Ranby Hall

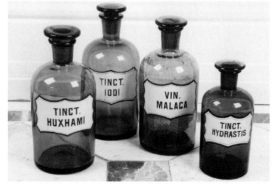

Circular Scent Bottle ▼

- *1902*

A circular scent bottle painted
with two Japanese ladies in
traditional dress embracing each
other, set against a background of
green foliage.
- *diameter 7cm*
- **£155**   • Trio

Square Scent Bottle ▼

- *circa 1890*

A square French scent bottle in
turquoise, fitted with a gold
stopper and chain. Decorated
with a gold floral design.
- *diameter 3cm*
- **£158**   • Trio

Oval Scent Bottle ▲

- *circa 1890*

An oval, Victorian scent bottle
in white porcelain, with a silver
stopper. Decorated with a red
butterfly, pink flowers and foliage.
- *height 6cm*
- **£158**   • Trio

Expert Tips

*When examining a bottle,
make sure that the glass is in
a non-chipped state and is
devoid of cracks. If there are
chips on the rim these can
sometimes be ground out.*

Enamel Scent Bottle ▲

- *circa 1890*

A white enamel scent bottle
decorated with pink flowers
and surmounted by filigree
work on a gold chain.
- *diameter 3cm*
- **£135**   • Trio

Victorian Scent Bottle ▲

- *circa 1890*

A Victorian, oval scent bottle
in clear glass, decorated with
gold flowers and fitted with a
pinch-back gold chain.
- *height 6cm*
- **£199**   • Trio

Bohemian Glass Bottle ▼
- *circa 1860*

Floral perfume bottle and large cut stopper in Bohemian glass, with enamelling.
- £300   • Trio

Red Glass Scent Bottle ▼
- *1920*

Art Deco perfume bottle in deep red glass, with a tassel and opaque glass stopper.
- *height 14cm*
- £168   • Trio

Jug-Shaped Scent Bottle ➤
- *1860*

A French ruby scent bottle in the shape of a stylised jug, with ruby stopper. Decorated with a gilt foliage design on the bottle and handle. The metal base carries a gilt foliage design.
- *height 12cm*
- £210   • Trio

Square Scent Bottle ▼
- *1930*

Square glass Art Deco perfume bottle, with a clear glass stopper and large grey silk tassel. Decorated with a black floral design.
- *height 10cm*
- £138   • Trio

Heart-Shaped Porcelain Bottle ▲
- *circa 1906*

A heart-shaped porcelain scent bottle, with a silver stopper. Decorated with a pair of eighteenth century figures.
- *diameter 4cm*
- £178   • Trio

Silver-Topped Bottle ▼
- *Georgian*
An early Georgian opaque scent bottle with silver top.
- *height 11cm*
- £178   • Trio

Stoneware Bottle ▼
- *circa 1647*
Whit stoneware bottle of bulbous proportions with handle, on a splayed base, inscribed with the words, "WHIT, 1647".
- *height 6cm*
- N/A   • Jonathan Horne

Victorian Scent Bottles ▲
- *1880*
Two Victorian cranberry- and vaseline-coloured scent bottles, together with their original leather carrying case.
- *height 14cm*
- £245   • Trio

English Scent Bottle ▲
- *1920*
English salmon-pink Art Deco perfume bottle, styled in the shape of a sailing boat with sail.
- *height 14cm*
- £150   • Trio

Green Scent Bottle ▶
- *circa 1890*
Green simulated vaseline glass scent bottle decorated with red and gold filigree with opaque glass stopper.
- *height 12cm*
- £110   • Trio

Clear Glass Bottle ▼
- *circa 1870*
A clear glass scent bottle elaborately decorated with ornate pinch beck. The stopper is painted with a scene of Church Street, Magdalene.
- *height 7.5cm*
- £188   • Trio

23

Cameras

Reflex Camera ▼
- *circa 1960*
Rolleiflex 2.8f twin lens reflex camera with built-in light meter and overhead viewfinder.
- £600
- Jessop Classic Photographica

Cine Camera ▼
- *circa 1960*
Bell & Howell "Sportster Standard 8" 8mm cine camera.
- £30
- Mac's Cameras

Kodak Field Camera ▲
- *circa 1950*
Kodak No.1 Autographic 120mm film field camera with folding case.
- £70
- Mac's Cameras

Filma Projector ▲
- *circa 1970*
Filma 240f 8mm sound projector. Standard 8 sound and silent. Portable and with outfit case.
- £100
- Mac's Cameras

35mm SLR Camera ▲
- *circa 1965*
Leicaflex 35mm SLR with f/2 semi-micron lens.
- £400
- Mac's Cameras

Expert Tips

The Leica camera totally dominated the 35mm market from the mid-1920s until the 1960s. Virtually any Leica camera will sell well at auction, the most avid collectors being the Japanese.

Rollei Camera ▼
- *circa 1975*
Rollei 35S gold 35mm camera. A specially finished precision compact camera. Limited edition of 1500, gold-plated.
- £900
- Jessop Classic Photographica

Field Camera ◄
- *circa 1930*
Deardorff 10x8-inch camera made of mahogany with nickel-plated fittings. Schneider and Symmar 300mm lens.
- £2,000
- Jessop Classic Photographica

Purma Roll Camera ➤

- *circa 1932*
Purma "Special" bakelite 127 roll camera with telescoping lens.
- £30
- Jessop Classic Photographica

Leicaflex SLR Camera ▲

- *circa 1970*
Leicaflex 35mm SLR camera with f2.8/90 Elmarit lens.
- £500
- Mac's Cameras

Hollywood Splicer ➤

- *circa 1960*
Hollywood stainless-steel splicer. 8mm x 16mm, in original box.
- £30
- Mac's Cameras

Flash-Bulb Holder ▲

- *circa 1949*
Leica Chico flash-bulb holder for Leica cameras.
- £20
- Jessop Classic Photographica

Mamiya 120 Camera ▼

- *circa 1970–1980*
Mamiya C33 first professional 120 camera with interchangeable lens. 6x6 image.
- £170   • Mac's Cameras

Expert Tips

Mint condition boxed originals are worth about double the price of the same camera showing reasonable wear. But the latter must be in perfect working order.

Roll Film Camera ▲

- *circa 1935*
Coronet midget 16mm camera made in five colours, blue being the rarest. Made in Birmingham.
- £350
- Jessop Classic Photographica

Miniature Spy Camera ➤

- *circa 1958*
Minox B sub miniature spy camera, which takes 8x11mm negatives. With brushed aluminium body.
- £180
- Jessop Classic Photographica

Light Exposure Meter ➤
- *circa 1960*
1 Kophot light exposure meter by Zeiss in a folding burgundy leather case.
- £30
- Mac's Cameras

Field Camera ▲
- *circa 1954*
MPP micro precision 5x4 press camera. Made in Kingston-upon-Thames, Surrey.
- £300
- Jessop Classic Photographica

Pyramid Tripod ➤
- *circa 1960*
Camera base with wooden legs and adjustable tubular metal stands.
- £15
- Mac's Cameras

Robot Camera ▲
- *circa 1940*
Luftwaffen Eigentum German Airforce robot camera. With built-in clockwork spring motor.
- £300
- Jessop Classic Photographica

Brownie Box Camera ▼
- *circa 1960*
Brownie Box camera, for 127 film, made in Canada by Kodak Eastman Co Ltd.
- £30
- Mac's Cameras

Cine Camera ▲
- *circa 1960*
A standard 8 film Bolex 8mm cine camera and a selection of Kern lenses with leather cases and original instructions.
- £100
- Mac's Cameras

Slide Projector ▲
- *circa 1960*
Aldis 35mm slide projector with original box.
- £30
- Mac's Cameras

Expert Tips

George Eastman's invention of the dry plate, in 1879, led to the mass production of cameras. The first Box Brownie was produced in 1888 and they changed almost imperceptibly for 80 years.

Quarter-Plate Camera ▲

- *circa 1935*
Baby speed graphic quarter plate camera. Made in America. With original leather straps.
- £400
- Jessop Classic Photographica

Autographic Camera ▲

- *circa 1920*
A Kodak vest pocket Autographic camera. Made in Rochester NY, USA.
- £30
- Mac's Cameras

Meopta Cine Camera ▼

- *circa 1958–65*
A standard 8 Meopta Admira 8mm cine camera with full metal case.
- £30
- Mac's Cameras

Mickey Mouse Camera ▼

- *circa 1980*
A 110 cartridge system camera with a plastic body in the form of Mickey Mouse. With viewfinder placed on forehead.
- £50
- Jessop Classic Photographica

Brownie 'Flash' Camera ▲

- *circa 1970*
A Brownie 'flash' 20 camera with interchangeable flash. With built-in filters. All plastic body in very good condition.
- £30
- Mac's Cameras

Expert Tips

Wet-plate cameras were manufactured from 1840–90 and are very rare. The craftsmanship of the case, as well as the manufacturer's name, define the value.

Square Roll Film Camera ▼

- *circa 1953*
First six V 120 6x6cm square roll film camera. One of the first to be made in Japan, inspired by earlier German designs.
- £100
- Jessop Classic Photographica

Cartridge System Camera ◄

- *circa 1975*
A 110 cartridge system camera modelled as a caricature of a British Airways Aeroplane. In good condition.
- £60
- Jessop Classic Photographica

Bolex 16mm Cine Camera ➤

- *circa 1960s*

Bolex 16mm cine camera, model number H16m, with a Swiss-made body and Som Berthiot 17–85mm zoom lens.
- *33cm x 21.5cm*
- £500 • Jessop Classic

Thornton Pickard Camera ▲

- *circa 1909*

Triple extension, Thornton Pickard camera which uses ½ plate-sized negatives (glass plates used, not films). Made of wood with leather bellows.
- *21cm x 25.5cm*
- £300 • Jessop Classic

Teleca Bino Camera ▼

- *1950*

Relatively rare, subminiature 16mm Teleca Bino camera, which is built into a pair of binoculars. Fitted with standard 10mm x 14mm lenses and supplied with a brown leather case.
- *10 x 9cm*
- £299 • Photo. Gallery

C8 Cine Camera ▼

- *1954*

Bolex Standard 8 cine camera with a clockwork windup and single interchangeable lens.
- *12.5cm x 6cm*
- £50 • Jessop Classic

Widelux Super Wide Angle Camera ▲

- *circa 1970s*

Widelux super wide angle viewfinder camera with an unusual rotating lens. The camera uses 120 film.
- *23cm x 28cm*
- £1,399 • Jessop Classic

Kodak Medallist II Rangefinder Camera ▲

- *1946–53*

Rare Kodak Medallist II rangefinder camera, fitted with an F3.5 100mm Ektar lens.
- *20cm x 13cm*
- £349 • Jessop Classic

Rollei 35 Camera   ▼

- *1971*

Gold Rollei 35 camera, supplied with a brown leather case and a red felt-lined wooden box. Fitted with an F3.5 Tessar lens.
- *9.5cm x 6cm*
- £899   • Jessop Classic

Kodak Retina II F, 35mm Camera   ▼

- *1963*

Kodak Retina II F, 35mm camera with an F2.8, 45mm Xenar lens. The built-in flash bulb holder is an unusual feature for this style of camera.
- *13cm x 8.5cm*
- £100   • Jessop Classic

Blair Stereo Weno with Case   ▶

- *1902*

Blair stereo Weno camera with case (as seen underneath), made in Rochester, New York. Supplied with a pair of Plastigmat lenses. Uses 116 Kodak film which has now been discontinued.
- *26.5cm x 11.5cm*
- £299   • Jessop Classic

Rollei Camera   ▲

- *1966–67*

Rollei 35 standard camera fitted with an F3.5 Tessar lens.
- *9.5cm x 6cm*
- £299   • Jessop Classic

Houghton Ticka Camera   ▲

- *1905–14*

Houghton Ticka Spy camera. This is designed to look like a pocket watch with an engraved monogram on the cover. The camera is hidden underneath the winding mechanism.
- *6.5cm x 5cm*
- £249   • Jessop Classic

Canon IV Camera   ▲

- *circa 1950s*

Canon IV range finder camera with detachable flash unit and a 50mm 1.9 Serenar lens. Supplied with a brown leather case. This model is based on a Leica design.
- *14cm x 7cm*
- £499   • Jessop Classic

Chess Sets

Ivory Chess Set ◄

- *circa 1845*
A rare 19th-century French
design ivory chess set.
- *height 10cm (king)*
- £8,500 • G.D. Coleman

Boxwood and Ebony
Staunton Chess Set ▲

- *late 19th century*
Mahogany green baize-lined lift-
top box with Jacques of London
green paper label to the inside lid.
- *height 19cm (king)*
- £950 • G.D. Coleman

Tortoiseshell & Ivory
Chess Set ◄

- *19th century*
Interlaced vine decoration on
light mahogany base.
- *height 19cm*
- £650 • Shahdad

Mythological Chess Set ►

- *circa 1920*
Unusual French decorated lead
chess set on a mythological
classical theme.
- *height 13cm (king)*
- £1,800 • G.D. Coleman

Selenus Chess Set ▲

- *circa 1800*
German carved bone with red
and white kings and queens
topped by Maltese crosses.
- *height 12cm*
- £2,850 • G.D. Coleman

Painted Metal Chess Set ▼

- *circa 1920*
King and queen representing
mythical gods. White figures
show a mottled effect.
- £1,800 • G.D. Coleman

Portuguese European
vs Chinese Chess Set ▲

- *circa 1865*
Fine carved ivory, from Macau.
- *height 10cm (king)*
- £1,850 • G.D. Coleman

Quartz Chess Set

- ***19th century***

An Indian rock crystal (quartz) export chess set with red and white colours.

- £1,250 • G.D. Coleman

Staunton Chess Set

- ***circa 1880***

Ivory Staunton chess set by Jaques of London with "Carton Pierre" casket and chess board.

- £2,500 • G.D. Coleman

Russian Ivory Chess Set

- ***19th century***

Carved and turned in mammoth ivory. One side natural, the other side with unusual pewter effect.

- *height 8.2cm (king)*
- £850 • G.D. Coleman

Wooden Chess Set

- ***19th century***

Very rare. All pieces are in the form of "The Bears of Berne". Made of Swiss natural wood, some stained darker.

- £2,850 • G.D. Coleman

Ivory Monobloc Set

- ***circa 1835***

Finely carved. One side in rare stained green, the other natural.

- *height 10.5cm (king)*
- £2,850 • G.D. Coleman

"Bauhaus" Wooden Chess Set

- ***early 20th century***

Chess set and board (not photographed).

- *height 10cm (king)*
- £380 • G.D. Coleman

Expert Tips

The modern era of chess dates from the 16th century, when the moves of the game began to take their present form. Philidor, a Frenchman who played in the 1700s, is widely regarded as the first world champion.

Staunton Ivory Set

- ***circa 1865***

Magnificent rare set by Jaques of London. With gold and red leather case and board.

- *height 14cm (king)*
- £16,500 • G.D. Coleman

American Chess Set ▼
- *1876*

American chess set in soft metal, signed "Le Mon" and dated 1876. Presented in its original box.
- *height 10cm/king*
- £3,500 • G.D. Coleman

German Chess Set ▲
- *1795*

German chess set of Selenus design, with black and white pieces in ivory.
- *height 8cm*
- £790 • G.D. Coleman

Coromandel Games Compendium ▲
- *circa 1880*

Coromandel games box in wood, containing chess, backgammon, checkers, cribbage, dominoes and draughts.
- *33cm x 20cm x 22cm*
- £1,900 • Langfords Marine

French Chess Set ▶
- *1800*

French chess set with pieces carved from lion wood and bone. Figures are black or red, both colours decorated with white edging.
- *height 8cm/king*
- £1,650 • G.D. Coleman

Expert Tips

The Victorian era (1837–1901) saw a great expansion in board games, and chess was no exception, and with the expansion of the British Empire pieces can be found from all over the world. The most celebrated designer of chess pieces is Jack Staunton whose work is of the Victorian era, and remains highly collectable.

Military Chess Set ◀
- *1870*

Chinese export ivory chess set based on the military theme of the Emperor Napoleon versus the Duke of Wellington.
- *height 10cm/king*
- £2,450 • G.D. Coleman

Bone Chess Set ▲
• 1840
English chess set in carved bone,
with figures in red and white.
• height 8cm/king
• £1,250　　• G.D. Coleman

French Ivory Chess Set ▲
• 1800
French ivory chess set, with one
side in natural ivory and one side
coloured in faded Shagrin green.
• height 9cm/king
• £1,750　　• G. D. Coleman

Silver Chess Set ▼
• 1970
English silver and silver gilt chess
set of rococo design bearing a
hallmark.
• height 9cm/ king
• £1,950　　• G.D. Coleman

Backgammon and Chess Set ▼
• 1840
Indian ivory chess and
backgammon set, with black and
natural ivory figures. Presented
in folding ivory chessboard box.
• 45cm x 50cm x 5cm
• £4,500　　• G.D. Coleman

Staunton Chess Set ▼
• 19th century
Ebony and boxwood chess set
made by Staunton, presented in
original box, by Jakes of London.
• height 9cm/king
• £480　　• G.D. Coleman

Commemorative Ware

Bone China Jug ◀
- *1888*
Continental bone china jug
commemorating the silver
wedding anniversary of Prince
Edward and Princess Alexandra.
- *height 12.5cm*
- £85   • Hope & Glory

Caricature Mug ▶
- *1991*
A caricature mug of the former
Prime Minister Margaret
Thatcher and her husband.
- *height 9cm*
- £33   • Hope & Glory

Queen Elizabeth II Bust ▼
- *1953*
Bust of Queen Elizabeth II to
commemorate her coronation in
1953, by Staffordshire Morloy.
- *height 18cm*
- £80   • Hope & Glory

Golden Jubilee Mug ▼
- *1887*
Small cream and blue mug,
commemorating the golden
jubilee of Queen Victoria.
Sold in the Isle of Wight.
- *height 6cm*
- £125   • Hope & Glory

Golden Jubilee Beaker ▲
- *1887*
Beaker commemorating the
golden jubilee of Queen Victoria,
showing young and old portraits.
Issued as a gift to school children
in Hyde Park.
- *height 10.5cm*
- £125   • Hope & Glory

Accession Jug ▲
- *1837*
Blue and white Accession
jug inscribed "Hail Victoria".
Showing a portrait of the young
Queen Victoria.
- *height 29cm*
- £1,275   • Hope & Glory

Coronation Mug ▼
- *1911*

Coronation mug of King George
V and Queen Mary.
- *height 7cm*
- £24   • Magpies

Loving Cup ▲
- *1937*

A bone china loving cup, by
Shelly, to commemorate the
proposed coronation of King
Edward VIII.
- *height 11.5cm*
- £275   • Hope & Glory

Poole Pottery Vase ▼
- *1977*

Vase commemorating the silver
jubilee of Queen Elizabeth II,
showing the lion and unicorn.
- *height 25cm*
- £125   • Hope & Glory

Musical Teapot ◄
- *circa 1953*

Teapot in the form of a coach,
commemorating the coronation
of Queen Elizabeth II. Plays the
National Anthem.
- *height 13cm*
- £240   • Hope & Glory

Winston S. Churchill Toby Jug ▼
- *circa 1941*

With anchor handle, by Fieldings,
representing Churchill's second
appointment as First Lord.
- *height 15cm*
- £190   • Hope & Glory

Pottery Mug ►
- *circa 1969*

A mug from the Portmerion
pottery to commemorate the first
landing of men on the moon by
Apollo II.
- *height 10cm*
- £70   • Hope & Glory

Snuffbox ►
- *1895*

Victorian silver table snuffbox,
inscribed as presented by HRH
Albert Edward of Wales.
- *length 14cm*
- £2,850 • S. & A. Thompson

Bone China Plate ▼
- *circa 1900*

By Royal Worcester to commemorate the relief of Mafeking. Transfer shows Baden-Powell.
- *diameter 23.5cm*
- £140   • Hope & Glory

Victorian Mug ▲
- *circa 1878*

Mug commemorating the visit of Edward, Prince of Wales, to India on the occasion of Queen Victoria being made Empress.
- *height 10.5cm*
- £150   • Hope & Glory

Four Castles Plate ▲
- *1901*

Black transfer on earthenware plate to commemorate the death of Queen Victoria, such items are quite scarce.
- *diameter 24.5cm*
- £240   • Hope & Glory

Dutch Delft Plaque ▼
- *circa 1945*

To commemorate the liberation of Holland. Showing mother, child and aeroplane.
- *height 20cm*
- £150   • Hope & Glory

Chocolate Tin ▲
- *circa 1953*

Royal blue enamelled tin with fleur de lys motif, commemorating the coronation of Queen Elizabeth II.
- *height 7cm*
- £5   • Magpies

Expert Tips

The market for commemorative items is driven by emotion. They start off overpriced and, as the individual becomes less well known, may lose value.

Officer on Horseback ▲
- *circa 1910*

German. Napoleonic period. Probably Dresden.
- *height 38cm*
- £2,500   • The Armoury

Pottery Loving Cup ➤
- *1897*

Loving cup by Brannum pottery, commemorating the Diamond Jubilee of Queen Victoria.
- *height 14cm*
- £240   • Hope & Glory

Whisky Decanter ▼

- *1911*

Spode decanter made for Andrew Usher & Co, distillers, Edinburgh, commemorating the coronation of George V.
- *height 25cm*
- £160   • Hope & Glory

Children's Plate ▼

- *1847*

Showing the young Edward, Prince of Wales, on a pony. Entitled "England's Hope".
- *diameter 16.5cm*
- £340   • Hope & Glory

Teapot ▶

- *circa 1897*

Commemorating the Diamond Jubilee of Queen Victoria. Copeland bone china with gold decoration. Portrait of Victoria in relief.
- *height 14cm*
- £525   • Hope & Glory

Pair of Perfume Flasks ▲

- *circa 1840*

Hand-decorated porcelain perfume flasks by Jacob Petit, commemorating the marriage of Queen Victoria and Prince Albert.
- *height 31cm*
- £3,750   • Hope & Glory

Ceramic Plaque ▲

- *circa 1911*

Plaque, by Ridgways, to commemorate the coronation of George VI and Queen Mary.
- *16 x 21cm*
- £85   • Hope & Glory

Coronation Mug ▼

- *1902*

Copeland mug commemorating the coronation of King Edward VII and Queen Alexandra. This mug shows the correct date of August 9th, 1902. Most commemorative ware gives the date as June 26th, from when the event was postponed due to the King's appendicitis.
- *height 7.5cm*
- £160   • Hope & Glory

Wedgwood Mug ▼

- *circa 1937*

A Wedgwood mug commemorating the coronation of King George VI, designed by Eric Ravilious.
- *height 11cm*
- £475   • Hope & Glory

Miners' Strike Plate ▲
- **1984**
Bone china plate to commemorate the great miners' strike of 1984–85. Issued by the National Union of Mineworkers.
- *diameter 27cm*
- **£58**   • Hope & Glory

Loving Cup ▲
- **1987**
Bone china loving cup by Royal Crown Derby. Commemorating the third term in office of Margaret Thatcher. Limited edition of 650.
- *height 7.75cm*
- **£160**   • Hope & Glory

Engagement Mug ▲
- **1981**
China mug depicting Prince Charles's ear. Drawn by Marc Boxer, made at the engagement of Charles and Diana.
- **£5**   • Hope & Glory

Victorian Cypher ▼
- **1890**
Victorian English carved wooden gesso royal cypher.
- *90cm x 65cm*
- **£2,500**   • Lacquer Chest

Jubilee Mug ▼
- **1935**
Ceramic mug celebrating the silver jubilee of King George V and Queen Mary.
- *height 7cm*
- **£24**   • Magpies

Royal Visit Teapot ▼
- **1939**
Teapot issued in commemoration of a royal visit to Canada made by George VI and Queen Elizabeth I in 1939.
- *height 13cm*
- **£85**   • Hope & Glory

Coalport Plate ▲
- 1897

Bone china plate issued by Coalport to commemorate Queen Victoria's diamond jubilee.
- *diameter 22cm*
- £140   • Hope & Glory

Pottery Folly ▲
- 1969

Caernarvon castle folly in Keystone pottery, issued to commemorate the investiture of Prince Charles in July 1969.
- *height 21cm*
- £65   • Hope & Glory

Coronation Cup and Saucer ▲
- 1902

Bone china cup and saucer commemorating the coronation of Edward VII. Made by Foley.
- *height 5.5cm*
- £58   • Hope & Glory

Boer War Egg Cups ▲
- 1900

Continental bone china egg cups depicting generals from the Boer War.
- *height 6.5cm*
- £60 each   • Hope & Glory

Birthday Mug ▲
- 1991

Bone china mug by Aynsley to commemorate the thirtieth birthday of Princess Diana.
- *height 9.5cm*
- £70   • Hope & Glory

Child's Plate ▲
- 1821

Very unusual child's plate depicting Queen Caroline.
- £325   • Hope & Glory

Bust of Wellington ◄
- *circa 1835*

Pre-Parian bust of Wellington in Felspar porcelain. Issued by Copeland and Garrett.
- *height 20cm*
- £290   • Hope & Glory

Coins & Medals

Commemorative Coin ▼
● *1935*
A gold coin commemorating the
Silver Jubilee of King George V.
The coin shows the King and
Queen Mary with Windsor Castle
on reverse.
● *diameter 31mm*
● £250 ● Malcolm Bord

Half-Sovereign Coin ▼
● *1817*
A gold King George III half-
sovereign coin.
● *diameter 19mm*
● £250 ● Malcolm Bord

Austrian Coin ▼
● *1936*
Gold Austrian 100-schilling coin
with Madonna on obverse and
Austrian shield on reverse.
● *diameter 32mm*
● £450 ● Malcolm Bord

Gold Guinea Coin ▲
● *1794*
A gold George III guinea coin.
This issue is known as the
"Spadge Guinea".
● *diameter 19mm*
● £200 ● Malcolm Bord

Gold Sovereign Coin ▼
● *1553*
Queen Mary fine sovereign coin
of thirty shillings. With Queen
enthroned and Tudor Rose on
reverse. Date in Roman numerals.
● *diameter 44mm*
● £5,000 ● Malcolm Bord

George III Crown ▲
● *1750*
A silver George III crown coin,
with the early head portrait.
● *diameter 38mm*
● £750 ● Malcolm Bord

Silver Penny ▲
● *circa 1025*
A short cross-type silver penny
from the court of King Cnut.
● *diameter 32mm*
● £100 ● Malcolm Bord

George III Guinea Coin ▼
● *1813*
A gold George III guinea coin.
This coin is known as the
"Military Guinea".
● *diameter 19mm*
● £800 ● Malcolm Bord

Order of the Indian Empire ◄

• 1900

Order of the Indian Empire Cie breast badge in case of award.

• £450　• Chelsea (OMRS)

Russian Medal ▼

• 1915

Imperial Russian Cross of St. George IV class.

• £45　• Chelsea (OMRS)

Great War Medal ▲

• 1911–37

A distinguished service order (George V) in Garrard & Co, in case of award.

• £450　• Chelsea (OMRS)

Miniature Medals ▼

• 1918

A set of KCMG, CB (Gold) group of ten miniatures attributed to Major General Sir Andrew Mitchell Stuart. Royal Engineers.

• £385　• Chelsea (OMRS)

Cap Badge ▲

• 1914–18

Royal Sussex Regiment silver and enamel officer's cap badge.

• £100　• Chelsea (OMRS)

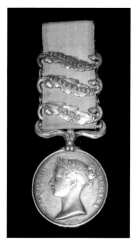

Crimea War Medal ▲

• 1854–56

A Crimea war medal from 1854, with three clasps, "Alma" "Inkermann" and "Sebastopol". Awarded to G. Bartlett of the 63rd Regiment.

• £350　• Chelsea (OMRS)

Expert Tips

The value of coins depends on their mint mark, design, date and condition, which is graded from FDC (fleur de coin or mint condition) to F (fair). Always have your collection photographed for insurance purposes, and store the information away from the collection.

Memorial Plaque ➤
- **1914**
Great War memorial plaque dedicated to Ernest George Malyon of the 2nd/16th Battalion London Regiment and inscribed "He died for freedom and honour".
- *diameter 12cm*
- **£25** • Chelsea (OMRS)

Military Clasp ▲
- **1943**
World War II German Navy U-boat Clasp for Bravery. Mid-war zinc example by Peeuhaus.
- **£575** • Chelsea (OMRS)

Leopold II Medal ▲
- **1915**
Order of Leopold II 2nd Class neck badge.
- **£175** • Chelsea (OMRS)

Waterloo Medal ▼
- **1815**
A Waterloo medal, 1815, awarded to Joseph Porch of the 11th Light Dragoons, wounded in action.
- **£1,000** • Chelsea (OMRS)

Cap Badge ▲
- **1939–45**
Royal Armoured Corps WWII plastic cap badge.
- **£25** • Chelsea (OMRS)

Air Force Medal ▼
- **1945**
A European Aircrew Star, awarded to a serving member of the Royal Air Force in World War II.
- **£105** • Chelsea (OMRS)

Military Medal Trio ▼
- **1918**
A trio of World War I medals, including the Victory medal, awarded to Private H. Codd of the East Yorkshire Regiment.
- **£35** • Chelsea (OMRS)

Ephemera

Thor ▾
- *January 1970*

The Mighty Thor, no. 172, original price one shilling, from Marvel Comics.
- £10   • Gosh

Famous Crowns Series ▾
- *1938*

Set of 25 cards, by Godfrey Phillips Ltd. Illustration shows an Italian crown.
- £8   • Murray Cards

Strange Tales ▶
- *1967*

Strange Tales no.161– *Doctor Strange – The Second Doom*. Published by Marvel Comics.
- £15
- Book & Comic Exchange

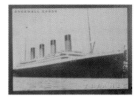

Titanic Series ▲
- *date 1999*

Set of 25 large-scale cards of the *Titanic*, produced by Rockwell Publishing at the time of James Cameron's film.
- £10   • Murray Cards

Star Trek ▲
- *1970*

Star Trek no.7 March 1970. Published by Gold Key.
- £50
- Book & Comic Exchange

Superman Series ▾
- *1968*

Set of cards, issued as series 950 by Primrose Confectionery Co, with sweet cigarettes. Illustration shows "Space Nightmare".
- £15   • Murray Cards

Kensitas Flower Series ▾
- *1933*

An unusual series of 60 cigarette collecting items with silk flowers enclosed in envelopes. By J Wix & Sons.
- £168   • Murray Cards

Ray Lowry Cartoon ▾
- *1992*

An original cartoon drawing by Ray Lowry.
- £65   • Gosh

Amazing Spiderman ▼
- *February 1966*
Amazing Spiderman no. 333 – *The Final Chapter!* – published by Marvel Comics.
- £50 • Gosh

Searle Lithograph ▼
- *circa 1960*
A Ronald Searle lithograph from "Those Magnificent Men in Their Flying Machines".
- £420 • Gosh

Romantic Story ▼
- *September 1958*
No. 40 – *Love's Tender Moments* – published by Charlton.
- £17.50 • Gosh

Opera Series ▲
- *1895*
Set of six opera cards, collected with products of The Liebig Extract Meat Co, France.
- £80 • Murray Cards

The Incredible Hulk ▲
- *September 1968*
The Incredible Hulk, issue no. 107, by Marvel Comics.
- £13.50 • Gosh

Billiard Series ▲
- *circa 1905*
Set of 15 cards of *double entendre* billiard terms, from Salmon & Gluckstein.
- £825 • Murray Cards

Monte Hale ▼
- *1952*
Monte Hale Western comic. Issue no. 76, price 10 cents.
- £15
- Book & Comic Exchange

Fantastic Four ▼
- *March 1966*
Issue no. 48 – *The X-Men!* – published by Marvel Comics.
- £225 • Gosh

Political Cartoon ▼
- *1997*
A political cartoon – *Springs in Spring* – by John Springs.
- £150 • Gosh

Stan Eales Cartoon ▲
- *1998*

A cartoon by Stan Eales of a man standing on the ledge of a burning building.
- £250   • **Cartoon Gallery**

Blakes 7 ▲
- *October 1981*

Blakes 7 magazine issue no. 1, published by Marvel UK.
- £8–12
- **Book & Comic Exchange**

The Dandy ▼
- *April 1973*

The Dandy, issue no. 1640, published by D.C. Thompson.
- £1   • **Gosh**

Strange Tales ▼
- *March 1964*

Strange Tales issue no. 118 – *The Human Torch* – published by Marvel Comics.
- £17   • **Gosh**

Playboy ◄
- *May 1969*

May 1969 issue of *Playboy* magazine, in good condition.
- £6   • **Radio Days**

Expert Tips

Most magazines launched run to only one issue, so that factor is no rarity. Condition must be excellent.

Marvel Masterworks ▲
- *1997*

Spiderman volume 1.
- £25   • **Gosh**

Cricket Series ▲
- *circa 1896*

Wills's first set of 50 cricketing cigarette cards. Illustration shows Dr W. G. Grace of Gloucestershire.
- £3,250   • **Murray Cards**

Soho International ▲
- *1971*

Volume 1, No. 1.
- £10
- **Book & Comic Exchange**

National Costumes Series ▼
- **1895**

Wills's cigarette cards set of 25. This card shows a Venetian beauty.

- **£4,125** • **Murray Cards**

X-Men ▼
- **January 1969**

X-Men magazine, issue no. 52 – *Armageddon Now!* – published by Marvel Comics.

- **£20** • **Gosh**

Famous Film Scene Series ▲
- **1935**

Set of 48 cigarette cards, by Gallaher Ltd. Shows Laurel & Hardy from "Babes in Toyland."

- **£36** • **Murray Cards**

Watchmen ▲
- **1987**

The collected edition of a comic original in 12 issues, retelling the super-hero story.

- **£14.95** • **Gosh**

Radio Times Cartoon ▼
- **1998**

A topical cartoon for *Radio Times* by Kipper Williams.

- **£120** • **Cartoon Gallery**

Mayfair Magazine ▼
- **1970**

Volume 3, no.1. British edition.

- **£20**
- **Book & Comic Exchange**

The Observer Cartoon ▼
- **1997**

Political cartoon by Chris Riddell, from *The Observer*.

- **£225** • **Cartoon Gallery**

Expert Tips

A good rule when starting to collect comics is to stick to a particular company, character or artist and collect everything to do with them before moving on.

Buffy the Vampire Slayer ▶
- **1999**

Mail order only. Premium Darkhorse publication.

- **£10**
- **Book & Comic Exchange**

Vogue ▲
- **November 1946**
A November 1946 copy of *Vogue* by Condé Nast.
- **£10**
- **Radio Days**

Builders of the British Empire Series ▲
- *circa 1929*
Set of 50 cards by J A Pattreiouex. Illustration shows General Gordon.
- **£135**   • **Murray Cards**

Studio International Art ▲
- **April 1964**
Issue of the art magazine.
- **£6**
- **Book & Comic Exchange**

Film Fun ➤
- **1957**
Issue no. 1971. Published by The Amalgamated Press.
- **£1.50**   • **Gosh**

Famous Monsters No. 46 ▲
- **1967**
Famous Monsters of Filmland.
- **£5–10**
- **Book & Comic Exchange**

Witchblade ▲
- **November 1996**
Issue no. 10. Published by Top Cow and signed by the artist.
- **£20**
- **Book & Comic Exchange**

Expert Tips

Cigarette cards were mostly made in the USA and English-speaking countries and peaked in the 1930s. Production stopped during the Second World War.

Beatles Series ▼
- *circa 1998*
A set of 10 cards in a limited edition of 2,000. The illustration shows Paul McCartney.
- **£5**   • **Murray Cards**

Batman in the Sixties ▼
- **1997**
T.V. series spin-off magazine, published by DC Comics.
- **£15**   • **Gosh**

Aircraft of the Royal Air Force ▲
- *1938*

Set of 50 cigarette cards from Players. Illustration shows Hawker Hurricane.
- *£45*
- • Murray Cards

Sunday Times Cartoon ▲
- *1997*

A cartoon for *The Sunday Times* by Nick Newman.
- *£120*
- • Cartoon Gallery

Roses Series ▲
- *1912*

Set of 50 cigarette cards from Wills. Illustration shows a Mrs Cocker Rose.
- *£50*
- • Murray Cards

Akira Comic ▼
- *1988*

Akira issue no. 2, by Epic publishers. Signed by the translator Frank Yonco.
- *£10*
- • Book & Comic Exchange

Boys' Ranch ▼
- *June 1951*

Boys' Ranch issue no. 5 – *Great Pony Express Issue* – published by Home Comics.
- *£45*
- • Gosh

Noted Cats Series ▼
- *1930*

Set of 24 cards by Cowans Confectionery, Canada. Shows a Persian male cat.
- *£132*
- • Murray Cards

Notable MPs ▼
- *1929*

Series of 50 cigarette cards of politicians, from Carreras Ltd. Illustration shows caricature of David Lloyd George.
- *£45*
- • Murray Cards

Custard Drawing ▼
- *1999*

A drawing of the character Custard, by Bob Godfrey, taken from the TV series "Roobarb".
- *£130*
- • Cartoon Gallery

Children of Nations Series ▼
- *circa 1900*

Set of 12 cards by Huntley & Palmer biscuit manufacturers, for sale in France.
- *£66*
- • Murray Cards

Konga ▾
- *1960*

An issue of *Konga* magazine, published by Charlton Comics.
- £15 • Gosh

Incredible Hulk ▾
- *1969*

Incredible Hulk, issue no. 112 – *The Brute Battles On!* – published by Marvel Comics.
- £12
- Book & Comic Exchange

Types of Horses ▾
- *1939*

Set of 25 large cigarette cards from John Player & Sons. Illustration shows a Cob horse.
- £85 • Murray Cards

Waterloo Series ▲
- *circa 1914*

Set of 50 cigarette cards from Wills, never issued from fear of offending the French during First World War.
- £4,750 • Murray Cards

Expert Tips

The French have been producing collectable cards – on products other than cigarettes – since the mid-19th century. Their point-of-sale power was unassailable.

Daredevil ➤
- *June 1964*

Daredevil issue no. 2, published by Marvel Comics.
- £135 • Gosh

Batman ▾
- *May 1942*

Very early *Batman* magazine – issue no. 10, by DC Comics.
- £220 • Gosh

Land Rover Series ▾
- *2000*

Set of seven cards, showing seven seater. Illustration shows 86-inch seven-seater.
- £3 • Murray Cards

Magical World of Disney ◄
- *circa 1989*

Set of 25 cards, from Brooke Bond tea. Illustration shows Mickey Mouse.
- £5 • Murray Cards

Robotech ▶
- 1985

The *Macross Saga* 7 issue, signed by the translator Frank Yonco with characteristic beard and glasses doodle. Published by Comico comics.
- £8
- Book & Comic

Mad Monsters ▼
- 1964

Issue No. 7 of comic *Mad Monsters*.
- height 30 cm
- £1.50
- Book & Comic

Zig Zag ◀
- 1976

Issue No. 65 of rock music magazine *Zig Zag*, with feature on the Beach Boys.
- £4
- Book & Comic

The Beano ◀
- 1969

Issue No. 1,405 of popular UK children's comic, *The Beano*.
- £1
- Book & Comic

The Dr Who Annual ▼
- 1979

1979 annual based on the cult TV series *Dr Who*.
- £5
- Book & Comic

Continental Film Review ▼
- *August 1968*

August 1968 issue of adult film magazine.
- £3
- Book & Comic

Bomp! ▲
- 1976–77

Music magazine *Bomp!*, featuring Brian Wilson.
- £5　　　● Book & Comic

Zeta ▲
- *1960s*

Issue No. 5, Volume 2, of erotic photography magazine *Zeta*.
- £10　　　● Book & Comic

Rolling Stone ◀
- *1970*

October 1970 issue of US rock music magazine *Rolling Stone*, featuring the life story of Janis Joplin.
- £6　　　● Book & Comic

Costume Prints ▼
- *1585*

A pair of prints by Nicolo Nicolai, depicting courtly figures in Ottoman costumes, displayed in handcrafted frames.
- *39cm x 29cm*
- £800　　　● Chelsea Gallery

Crawdaddy ▲
- *July 1973*

US music magazine *Crawdaddy*, featuring Marvin Gaye.
- £4　　　● Book & Comic

Gent ▼
- *1961*

Men's magazine *Gent*, featuring interviews with Mark Russell and Klaus Rock.
- £8　　　● Book & Comic

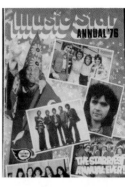

Music Star ▲
- **1976**

1976 annual of teenage pop magazine *Music Star*.
- £4   • Book & Comic

Continental Film Review ▲
- **March 1962**

March 1962 issue of *Continental Film Review*, featuring Brigitte Bardot on the cover.
- £4   • Book & Comic

International Times ▼
- **1974**

Issue No. 2, Volume 2, of UK underground newspaper *International Times*.
- £1.50   • Book & Comic

Shadow Hawk ▲
- **1992**

A first copy of the comic, with a glossy cover.
- *height 30cm*
- £2   • Book & Comic

The Lone Ranger ▲
- **1958**

The Lone Ranger comic book published by Gold Key.
- £6   • Book & Comic

Interview ▶
- **1977**

Newspaper format of Andy Warhol's magazine, *Interview*.
- £18   • Book & Comic

Kitchenalia

Bell Weight ▼

- *circa 1890*

A Victorian, two pound, solid brass kitchen weight in very good condition.

- *height 11cm*
- £22 • Magpies

Glass Cloche ▼

- *circa 1860*

A French glass cloche from the mid 19th-century.

- *diameter 55cm*
- £150 • Gabrielle de Giles

Pie Funnel ▲

- *circa 1890*

Roe's patent "Rosebud" ceramic pie funnel, with name on obverse and baking instructions on reverse.

- *height 8cm*
- £26 • Magpies

Scales ▲

- *circa 1940*

Berkel cast iron scales with red enamel finish, spirit level and adjustable foot. Weighs up to 2lb. Made in England.

- *height 50cm*
- £95 • After Noah

Chocolate Jug ▼

- *circa 1946*

Cadbury's salt glaze chocolate jug, hand-painted with the Cadbury's name and logo.

- *height 15cm*
- £22 • Magpies

Chamber-Stick ▼

- *circa 1890*

A late Victorian blue enamel chamber candlestick, with no chips to the enamel.

- *diameter 14cm*
- £12.50 • Magpies

Stone Sink ◀

- *circa 1890*

A late Victorian stone sink, with brown glaze to the interior and decorative glaze to the exterior.

- *length 95cm*
- £120 • Curios

Copper & Brass Urn ▲
- *circa 1820*
Copper and brass urn with brass tap and double-ring handle, banding and finial on a brass pedestal foot.
- *height 48cm*
- £250 • **Rosemary Conquest**

Expert Tips

In order to retain their value, it is important that items of kitchenalia should not be purely decorative. They must be complete and in working order.

Herb Chopper ▼
- *circa 1880*
A Victorian double-handled herb chopping knife.
- *length 24cm*
- £15 • **Magpies**

Fish Kettle ▶
- *circa 1900*
French copper fish kettle of three interlocking pieces.
- *length 53cm*
- £150 • **Youlls**

Cordial Syphon ▼
- *circa 1934*
Fluted, etched glass cordial syphon with brass top.
- *height 30cm*
- £20 • **Magpies**

Knife Sharpener ▶
- *circa 1890*
A Victorian patent knife sharpener with a cast-iron frame.
- *height 34cm*
- £475 • **Drummonds**

Salt Tin ▲
- *circa 1930*
White enamel tin for salt, with black lettering and detailing and domed lid.
- *height 26cm*
- £18 • **Magpies**

Flat Iron ◀
- *circa 1890*
Victorian cast-iron flat iron for use with cooking range.
- *length 13cm*
- £14 • **Magpies**

Butcher's Block ➤
- *circa 1860*

A 19th-century butcher's block and table with fluted pillars to the front and two cupboards.
- *height 84cm*
- **£1,625**   • Drummonds

Butcher's Block ▲
- *circa 1910*

Well worn English butcher's block with steel mounts.
- *height 75cm*
- **£170**   • Myriad

Watering Can ▼
- *circa 1880*

Decorative brass watering can with lattice design, hinged lid and two handles.
- *height 27cm*
- **£45**   • Magpies

Toaster ◄
- *circa 1930*

A manually-operated toaster made of chrome and painted metal, with bakelite knobs.
- *height 20cm*
- **£55**   • H. Hay

Teapot ▼
- *circa 1930*

Dartmouth Pottery teapot, with small white dots on a blue ground.
- *height 17cm*
- **£38**   • Magpies

Copper Funnel ▼
- *circa 1900*

A Victorian copper funnel with removable sieve.
- *height 12cm*
- **£18**   • Magpies

Steel Footman ◄
- *circa 1800*

Steel footman, for cooking, with cabriole legs on spade feet.
- *height 30cm*
- **£200**   • Albany

Novelty Egg Cups ◄
- *circa 1930s*

A group of novelty egg cups, showing cockerel, duck, owl and elephant.
- **from £9**
- **Magpies**

Teapot ▼
- *circa 1932*

A "Domino" teapot by T. G. Green, decorated with white dots on a blue ground.
- *height 12cm*
- **£55**
- **Magpies**

Biscuit Barrel ▲
- *circa 1930s*

A novelty Crown Derby biscuit barrel, in the shape of a dog, with black and white detailing, a red nose, brown collar and eyes and a yellow hat doubling as a top.
- *height 24cm*
- **£185**
- **Beverley**

Marmalade Jar ▲
- *circa 1900*

A late Victorian, two-tone stoneware jar for storing marmalade or preserves. Originally with cork stopper.
- *height 21cm*
- **£11**
- **Magpies**

Mortar & Pestle ▼
- *circa 1900*

A mortar and pestle, by Mason's, with turned wooden pestle and white ceramic mortar with crest. For grinding spices.
- *height 10cm*
- **£35**
- **Magpies**

Expert Tips

Much kitchenalia is to be found in boot fairs, jumble sales or junk shops. The advantage of junk shops is that they will probably have bought up the entire contents of a house for an agreed price and with the intention of acquiring one or two good items – anything that the vast range of other items fetches is "found" money for them and good value for you.

Watering Can ▲
- *circa 1860*

19th-century brass watering can with banding and hinged flap.
- *height 39cm*
- **£115**
- **Castlegate**

Bread Knife ►
- *circa 1900*

A late Victorian bread knife with a stainless steel, serrated blade and a fruitwood handle carved with the word "Bread".
- *length 31cm*
- **£12**
- **Magpies**

Scales ➤
- *circa 1940*
Berkel cast iron scales with red enamel finish and spirit level. Weighs up to 2lbs. Made in London.
- *length 50cm*
- **£95**   • After Noah

Chamber Stick ▲
- *circa 1910*
An Edwardian, enamelled chamber candlestick with floral decoration on a white ground with black, enamel rim.
- *diameter 14cm*
- **£14.50**   • Magpies

Expert Tips

Genuine, practical kitchen and scullery implements tend to be very plain and unfussy. Too much decoration may indicate a later copy.

Cocoa Tin ▼
- *circa 1890*
A Dutch cocoa tin, inscribed "Cacao C.J. Van Houten & Zoon. Weesp (Holland)", with profusely decorated panels.
- *height 31cm*
- **£110**   • Rosemary Conquest

Water Jug ◄
- *circa 1880*
Copper water jug with large splayed lip and tubular handle.
- *height 30cm*
- **£46**   • Magpies

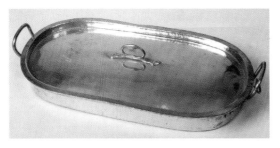

Rectangular Bread Bin ▼
- *circa 1930*
A rectangular bread bin, enamelled in white, with black lettering and detailing and blue enamelled handles.
- *height 30cm*
- **£34**   • Magpies

Copper Kettle ▼
- *circa 1870*
A Victorian copper kettle with slender, hooped handle.
- *height 31cm*
- **£105**   • Castlegate

Fish Kettle ◄
- *circa 1880*
A large, 19th-century copper fish kettle, with rounded ends and two handles.
- *height 19cm*
- **£135**   • Castlegate

Butcher's Block ➤
- *circa 1890*

A French bow-fronted butcher's block table with drawers and cupboards below.
- *length 36cm*
- **£2,850**   • **Drummonds**

Toaster ▲
- *circa 1959*

Early classic chrome toaster, by Morphy Richards. Immaculate condition.
- *height 19cm*
- **£58**   • **H. Hay**

Flour Jar ▲
- *circa 1950*

A white ceramic flour jar with red banded decoration around middle and on the finial top and broad red band to base.
- *height 16cm*
- **£32**   • **Magpies**

Copper Jug ▼
- *circa 1890*

Water jug in hammered copper, with large splayed lip and armorial frieze.
- *height 26cm*
- **£33**   • **Magpies**

Expert Tips

Even if your kitchenalia isn't worth much, it can still be useful. Redundant graters, for instance, with just the insertion of a candle, make excellent patio lights.

Flour Tin ▼
- *circa 1920*

White enamel flour tin with black lettering and detailing and black enamel on the two handles.
- *height 28cm*
- **£28**   • **Magpies**

Ovaltine Mug ▼
- *circa 1950*

Mug promoting the bedtime drink Ovaltine. These mugs were produced in association with their long-running radio show.
- *height 11cm*
- **£15**   • **Magpies**

Bottle Opener ◄
- *circa 1920*

A highly collectable Edwardian novelty bottle-opener in the shape of a lady's shoe, made of copper on cast iron.
- *length 12cm*
- **£27**   • **Magpies**

Potato Cutter ▼

- *1940*

The New "Villa" French fried potato cutter supplied in its original box.
- *26cm x 12cm x 12cm*
- £14   • Radio Days

Mini-Sweeper ▲

- *1940*

Mini-sweeper presented in its original box.
- *20cm x 14cm*
- £12   • Radio Days

Cream Maker ▼

- *1950s*

Bakelite and glass cream maker with alloy handle.
- *height 21cm*
- £15   • Kitchen Bygones

Enamelled Bread Bin ▲

- *1940s*

English enamelled bread bin with the letters in stylised font.
- *height 50cm*
- £25   • Kitchen Bygones

Cornish Ware Mug ▼

- *1940*

Cornish ware mug decorated with blue and white hoops.
- *height 8cm*
- £10.50   • Magpies

Glass Creamer ▼

- *1940*

Jubilee model glass hand-creamer with primrose yellow plastic cup and handle designed by Bel.
- *height 22cm*
- £16   • After Noah (KR)

Bakelite Thermos ▾
• *1930*
English green Bakelite thermos
with metal handle.
• *height 34cm*
• £11   • Magpies

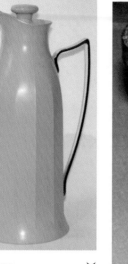

Squeezer ▾
• *1950s*
Solid aluminium vegetable or
fruit squeezer made by Atlantic.
• *height 20cm*
• £15   • Kitchen Bygones

Egg Timer ▾
• *Victorian*
Victorian egg timer with wood-
turned column and original
glass reservoir.
• *height 14cm*
• £15   • Kitchen Bygones

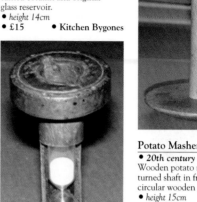

Potato Masher ▲
• *20th century*
Wooden potato masher with
turned shaft in fruitwood on a
circular wooden base.
• *height 15cm*
• £15   • Kitchen Bygones

Rolling Pin ▲
• *1950s*
Good quality wooden rolling pin
with turned painted handles.
• *length 40cm*
• £10   • Kitchen Bygones

Terracotta Bread Bin ▲
• *20th century*
Terracotta bread bin, with lid
and carrying handles.
• *height 33cm*
• £65   • Kitchen Bygones

Sugar Sifter ▼
- *circa 1930s*

Sugar sifter by T.G. Green, with blue and white banding.
- *height 28cm*
- £58   • Magpies

Bean Slice ▼
- *1920*

Iron bean slice with a brass handle, produced by Alexander Ware.
- £12   • Magpies

Copper Jelly Moulds ◄
- *circa 1900*

Set of three copper jelly moulds in the shape of oven-ready chickens. Used for making savoury jellies and patés.
- £14   • Magpies

Metal Funnel ▼
- *1940*

Blue enamelled metal funnel with handle.
- *height 17cm*
- £8.50   • Magpies

Ceramic Rolling Pin ▲
- *1950*

Ceramic white rolling pin with green handles, inscribed "Nutbrowne".
- *length 41cm*
- £25   • Magpies

Food Storage Flask ►
- *1930s*

A vacuum flask for food storage with eagle clasping the world.
- *height 38cm*
- £40   • Kitchen Bygones

Baker's Paddle ▼
- *1920*

A baker's folding paddle with spatulate head.
- *length 185cm*
- £45   • Kitchen Bygones

Brass Saucepot △

- *1910*

Sauce pot made of brass with iron handles and copper rivets.

- *height 6cm*
- £45 • Magpies

Larder Chest △

- *1890*

French Provincial larder chest consisting of four drawers and a cupboard. The whole resting on ogée bracket feet. With original distressed condition.

- *120cm x 90cm*
- £880 • Myriad

Circular Mould ▽

- *1880*

Ring-shaped brass jelly mould.

- *diameter 7cm*
- £24 • Magpies

Hexagonal Mould ▷

- *1890*

Hexagonal-shaped jelly mould in copper.

- *height 11.5cm*
- £11 • Magpies

Weighing Scales ◁

- *1940*

Horseshoe-shaped Swedish scales in bronze with enamelled dial and original weighing dish.

- *height 30cm*
- £54 • Magpies

Ink Filler △

- *1890*

Copper ink filler fitted with a side handle and a slender copper funnel, used for filling inkwells.

- *height 16cm*
- £35 • Magpies

Shirt-Sleeve Board △

- *1920*

Shirt-sleeve ironing board.

- *length 57cm*
- £25 • Kitchen Bygones

Cider Jar ◁

- *1940s*

Stoneware cider jar.

- *height 35cm*
- £25 • Kitchen Bygones

Expert Tips

It is a marvel how items like these can cast a spell over kitchens, cosy restaurants or bistros. Take care to remember that condition and an attractive patina is the key to success.

Luggage

Leather Trunk ◄
- *circa 1910*
Small Edwardian trunk of heavy-duty leather with wooden base slats and reinforced corners, sturdy brass catches and locks and two leather restraining straps with fitted loops. Carrying handles are fitted to the middle and to each end. The interior is lined with cotton ticking, compartmentalized and fitted with restraining straps.
- *length 79cm*
- £70–£150 • Henry Gregory

Crocodile Case ▼
- *circa 1928–29*
Crocodile case from Garrards of London, made from skin of animal shot by Captain S. J. Bassett in Zanzibar in 1926. With padded satin lining.
- *37cm x 25cm*
- £1,500 • Holland & Holland

Picnic Case for Two ▼
- *circa 1910*
English Edwardian leather picnic case, fully fitted with custom-made accoutrements, including chrome-finished hip flask, food storage containers, original Thermos flask, complete bone-handled set of stainless steel cutlery and china crockery.
- *width 28cm*
- £550 • Mia Cartwright

Picnic Hamper ▲
- *circa 1940*
Made from leather, cane and canvas, with iron fittings and large rope handles at either end.
- *length 75cm*
- £480 • Myriad Antiques

Suitcases ▲
- *1910*
Classic English leather suitcases with brass catches and locks and leather carrying-handles and lined interiors.
- £70 & £150
- Henry Gregory

Victorian Hat Case ▼
- *circa 1870*
Victorian hat case in hide leather with brass fittings and red quilted interior. Designed to carry two top hats and an opera hat.
- *height 87cm*
- *width 85cm*
- £475 • Mia Cartwright

Hat Box ◄
- *circa 1920*
Luxury leather hat box, holding several hats, with canvas lining and original travel sticker and initials "K.C." to front. Made in Northampton.
- *width 83cm*
- £375 • Matthews

Hat Box ▼

- *circa 1870*

Victorian leather hat box with brass fittings and leather handle.
- *35cm x 28cm x 30cm*
- £245   • Henry Gregory

Collar Box ▼

- *circa 1900*

Leather collar box in the shape of a horseshoe
- *18cm x 17cm x 8cm*
- £48   • Henry Gregory

Top Hat and Box ▲

- *circa 1850*

English leather box for a top hat, with brass fittings and leather strap, with red velvet lining. Complete with hat.
- *38cm x 22cm 35cm*
- £290   • Henry Gregory

Gun Case ▼

- *circa 1900*

English leather gun case with brass fittings and leather handle, having leather straps with brass buckle.
- *84cm x 23cm x 9cm*
- £490   • Henry Gregory

Expert Tips

Old luggage carries an air of sophistication and hints at a decadent past.

Travelling Trunk ▼

- *1850*

English leather brass-studded and bound travelling trunk.
- *42cm x 91cm x 46cm*
- £400   • Tredantiques

Mail Bag ▶

- *circa 1900*

Country house leather mail case with brass fixtures,
- *30cm x 25cm*
- £120   • Henry Gregory

Leather Gladstone Travelling Bag ◀

- *circa 1870*

All-leather Gladstone bag with brass attachments, two straps and double handles.
- *length 69cm*
- £480   • Henry Gregory

Mechanical Music

Polyphon Table Model Style 45 ▲
- *circa 1900*
Two-comb, Polyphon Sublime Harmony Piccolo, in superb carved walnut case with floral marquetry. With ten discs.
- £4,950   • Keith Harding

Twelve-Air Musical Box ▶
- *circa 1890*
Exceptionally good Nicole Frères 12-air, two-per-turn, forte-piano musical box, serial number 46094. Outstandingly beautiful case with exquisite marquetry on lid and front. Excellent tone and good musical arrangements of a popular operatic and light classical programme.
- £5,500   • Keith Harding

Miniature Musical Box ▼
- *circa 1890*
Two-air music box with the rare tunecard of AMI RIVENC. In fruitwood case inlaid with parquetry. Geneva.
- £750   • Keith Harding

Musical Ballerina ◀
- *circa 1890*
Automaton ballerina, rotating and dancing arabesques. On red plush base. By Rouillet et Decamps.
- £4,500   • Keith Harding

Swiss Musical Box ▲
- *circa 1850*
Swiss musical box of eight tunes. Inlaid with song bird and foliage decoration.
- £3,250   • Pendulum

Portable Gramophone ▲
- *circa 1920*
A Japanese portable gramophone, by Mikkephone, with unusual flattened horn speaker and carrying-case with strap.
- *width 30cm*
- £200   • TalkMach

Cylinder Piano ▲
- *circa 1860*
Small upright domestic piano. Rosewood case with red-cloth frontal, by Hicks of London and Bristol. With 10 tunes.
- £3,300   • Keith Harding

Musical Box ◄
- *circa 1865*
Forte Piano by Nicole Frères of Geneva, with eight operatic airs.
- **£4,995** • **Keith Harding**

Art Nouveau Polyphon ▼
- *circa 1900*
A rare autochange polyphon, from Leipzig, Germany, with 16 22-inch discs and orchestral bells in an Art Nouveau, mahogany case.
- **£9,500** • **Keith Harding**

Phonograph ▲
- *circa 1900*
An English "Puck" phonograph with large speaker.
- *height 35cm*
- **£250** • **TalkMach**

Musical Decanter ▲
- *circa 1835*
A very rare musical decanter of Prussian shape, with a Swiss movement. Plays two tunes.
- **£1,250** • **Jasmin Cameron**

Lecoultre Musical Box ▲
- *circa 1890*
Musical box in a rosewood case, with original key. Plays six dance tunes, listed on original card.
- **£2,400** • **Keith Harding**

Chiming Table Clock ➤
- *circa 1875*
Large chiming clock, in fruitwood with gilt brass mounts. Plays Westminster chimes on gongs, Whittington on bells.
- **£3,500** • **Keith Harding**

Musical Box ◄
- *circa 1895*
Nicole Frères key-wind musical box, playing eight Scottish airs. Rosewood lid with good marquetry in wood and enamel.
- **£3,950** • **Keith Harding**

English Organette ➤
- *circa 1910*

By J. M. Draper, England.
Fourteen notes, with three stops,
flute, expression and principal
which operate flaps over the reed
box to control the tone.
- £950 • Keith Harding

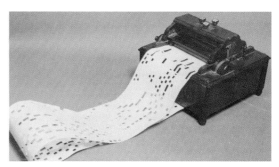

Phonograph Cylinders ▲
- *circa 1900*

Three phonograph cylinders, two
from Edison and one from Bell, in
their original packaging.
- £25–45 • TalkMach

Concert Roller Organ ▲
- *circa 1900*

Twenty-key organette by
Autophone Company, N.Y.
Played by "cobs" or barrels. Ten
cobs supplied.
- £1,750 • Keith Harding

Polyphon Table Model ▲
- *circa 1890*

Rare, style 48, with two combs.
Sublime Harmony accompanied
by Twelve Saucer Bells. Supplied
with eight discs in a walnut case.
- £5,800 • Keith Harding

Faventia Spanish Street Piano ▼
- *circa 1900*

Two barrels, each playing six
tunes. With red-grained finish, on
original green and yellow cart.
- £1,495 • Keith Harding

English Gramophone ◄
- *circa 1915*

An English gramophone by
HMV, "His Master's Voice Junior
Monarch".
- *height 36cm*
- £3,500 • Keith Harding

Expert Tips

*The Edison Gem and Edison
Standard phonographs were
produced in vast quantities.
Condition needs to be very good
to excite the collector.*

Dog Model Gramophone ◄
- *circa 1900*

By the Gramophone and
Typewriter company. Model
number 3. With original brass
horn and concert soundbox.
Completely overhauled.
- £1,950 • Keith Harding

Miscellaneous

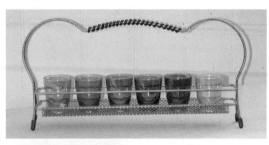

Harlequin Glass Cocktail Set ▲
- **1950**
Harlequin glass cocktail set with brass holder, plastic feet and roped handle.
- *18cm x 35cm*
- £25 • Radio Days

Expert Tips

Rubber items will remain well preserved if sprinkled with French chalk.

Victorian Cigar Case ▲
- *circa 1900*
A Victorian crocodile skin cigar case with silver trim.
- *length 15cm*
- £495 • The Reel Thing

American Handbag ▲
- **1940**
An American fabric and bamboo handbag with scrolled design.
- *24cm x 28cm*
- £150 • Linda Bee

Card Case ▼
- **1870**
Attractive, small crocodile skin card case.
- £125 • The Reel Thing

Royal Doulton Mug ▲
- *20th century*
A Royal Doulton mug naturalistically moulded as an R.A.F. pilot from World War II.
- *height 15cm*
- £65 • London Antique

Tortoiseshell Letter Opener ➤
- **1911**
Tortoiseshell letter opener with coins inserted.
- *length 20.5cm*
- £85 • Abacus Antiques

Tortoiseshell Comb ▼
- *1880*
Large tortoiseshell comb
for hair.
- *height 16cm*
- £95   • Abacus Antiques

Edwardian Shop Scales ▼
- *March 15th, 1906*
Early twentieth-century shop
scales inscribed "London &
Manchester". Made by the
Automatic Scale Company of
London & Manchester.
- *33cm x 60cm*
- £125   • Drummonds

English Crocodile Skin Bag ➤
- *1920*
An English stitched, deep
grained, box-shaped, brown
crocodile bag with a
monogrammed top.
- *42cm x 60cm*
- £150   • John Clay

Edla Fan and Humidifier ▼
- *1930s*
A French Art Deco bakelite fan
and humidifier,with a central
circular metal cover.
- *height 35cm*
- £200   • Decodence

Alligator Skin Bag ▼
- *1920*
An English stitched alligator skin
bag with leather handles.
- *55cm x 37cm*
- £175   • John Clay

Hair Grip ▲
- *circa 1900*
Early twentieth century
tortoiseshell hair grip.
- *height 13cm*
- £65   • Abacus Antiques

Eye Glass ▲
- *1920*
Tortoiseshell eye glass.
- *height 13cm*
- £25   • Abacus Antiques

Propeller Clock
- *circa 1917–18*
An Hispana Suiza working clock
mounted on a mahogany
propeller from a Sopworth
Dolphin Scout airplane.
- *260cm x 26cm x 17cm*
- £1,780 • Henry Gregory

Bakelite Comb ◀
- *1920*
A French Art Deco bakelite
hair comb.
- *length 14cm*
- £55 • Linda Bee

Milk Churn ▼
- *1890*
A galvanised steel milk churn of
unusual shape with floral garland
and swag decoration.
- *height 65cm*
- £380 • Myriad

Card Case ▲
- *1880*
A pink mother-of-pearl card case
decorated with birds.
- *height 9cm*
- £155 • Japanese Gallery

Perpetual Calendar ◀
- *20th century*
An early twentieth century
English perpetual calendar.
- £85 • North West 8

Barrel Decanter ▶
- *1880*
Walnut barrel decanter.
- *20cm x 6cm*
- £825 • Langfords Marine

American Handbag ▼
- *1960*

An American handbag made from black velvet with gold metal geometrical bands and shiny black perspex handle and lid.
- *20cm x 17cm*
- £150   • Linda Bee

Lizard Skin Handbag ▼
- *1950*

A 1950s classic black lizard skin bag.
- *24cm x 37cm*
- £95   • Linda Bee

Beehive ◄
- *1890*

A most unusual English beehive. with original basket work with wooden finial.
- *height 70cm*
- £120   • Myriad

Crocodile Handbag ►
- *1940*

A 1940s classically elegant Argentinian crocodile skin handbag with brass trim.
- *23cm x 28cm*
- £195   • Linda Bee

Pack of Cigarettes ▲
- *1940*

Original 1940s cigarettes branded "Dandy, Special Virginia".
- £20   • Linda Bee

Poodle Handbag ▼
- *1950*

A fun American handbag in laminated fabric with poodles on the front.
- *19cm x 28cm*
- £125
- Linda Bee

World War I Truncheon ▼
- *circa 1915*

World War I reserve truncheon with leather strap.
- *38cm x 4cm*
- £160   • Henry Gregory

Paperweights

American "Cherries" ▲
- *late 19th century*

American glass paperweight with central cherry pattern on a white latticino ground.
- *diameter 7cm*
- £620 ● G.D. Coleman

Expert Tips

The most collectable of glass paperweights were made between 1845 and 1849 at the French factories in Clichy, Baccarat and St Louis – all well represented here.

Clichy Blue Swirl ▼
- *1848*

A rare Clichy swirl glass paperweight in blue and white with central pink and white cones.
- *diameter 7cm*
- £1,350 ● G.D. Coleman

St Louis Paperweight ➤
- *circa 1855*

A St Louis glass paperweight with a mauve, dahlia flower pattern with green leaves.
- *diameter 8cm*
- £1,350 ● G.D. Coleman

Paul Ysart Paperweight ▼
- *circa 20th century*

Quality paperweight by Paul Ysart with a PY signature cane.
- *diameter 8cm*
- £480 ● G.D. Coleman

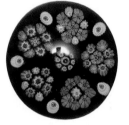

Baccarat Blue Primose ▼
- *circa 1850*

Baccarat glass paperweight showing a blue primrose and leaves on a clear ground with star cut base. Good condition.
- *diameter 5.5cm*
- £1,250 ● G.D. Coleman

Baccarat Scrambled ▲
- *circa 1850*

Paperweight of a type called "End of Day", since they were made after hours by glass workers with leftovers from the floor.
- *diameter 8cm*
- £580 ● G.D. Coleman

Green Jasper ▲
- *circa 1860*

Mid-19th-century St Louis paperweight with flowers on a green jasper ground.
- *diameter 6cm*
- £380 ● G.D. Coleman

Baccarat Pansy
- *circa 1850*

French Baccarat paperweight, inset with a red pansy and green foliage, on stonecut base.
- *diameter 5.5cm*
- £680 • G.D. Coleman

Bohemian Magnum ▼
- 1890

Glass hexagonal paperweight with an etched glass coat of arms with amber faceted flank.
- *11.5cm*
- £380 • G.D. Coleman

Baccarat Sulphite ▼
- 1976

Baccarat sulphite paperweight in facetop form, faceted with six lozenge cuts printed with a bust of Queen Elizabeth II.
- *diameter 7cm*
- £1,670 • London Antique

Floral St Louis ▲
- 1850

St Louis paperweight with pink floral cone design.
- *diameter 6.5cm*
- £7,850 • G.D. Coleman

Wedgwood Plaque ▲
- 1977

Glass paperweight with Wedgwood plaque of Queen Elizabeth II.
- *diameter 7cm*
- £150 • London Antique

Faceted Baccarat ▶
- 1976

Baccarat sulphite paperweight in facetop form. Faceted with six lozenge cuts printed with a bust of Prince Charles.
- *diameter 7cm*
- £2,670 • London Antique

Sturbridge ▼
- *circa 1880*

English Sturbridge Victorian concentric paperweight with multi-coloured cane design.
- *diameter 8cm*
- £380 • G.D. Coleman

Photographs

Coronation Photograph ▲
- *12th May 1937*
George VI coronation photograph, by Dorothy Wilding. Autographed by the King and Queen Elizabeth.
- £2,000   • The Armoury

Silver Gelatin Print ▲
- *20th century*
Photograph "Andy, Bob & Elvis" by Nat Finkelstein.
- *length 11.5cm*
- £550
- Photographers' Gallery

Colour Fresson Print ▼
- *1996*
New York colour Fresson print by Delores Marat.
- *length 45cm*
- £800
- Photographers' Gallery

Cyanotype Photograph ▼
- *20th century*
Plate entitled "Large Anenome" by Sheva Fruitman.
- *length 15cm*
- £325
- Photographers' Gallery

C-Type Colour Print ▲
- *20th century*
Adam Barfos, "Conference Building Elevators", from his International Territory series.
- *length 50cm*
- £1,000
- Photographers' Gallery

Silver Gelatin Print ▲
- *1951*
"Maidens in Waiting, Blackpool". One of a series by Bert Hardy.
- £500
- Photographers' Gallery

Expert Tips

It may seem facile to advise against damp and direct sunlight with regard to vintage photographs, but these are largely the reasons for their scarcity.

French Photograph Album ➤
- *circa 1890*
Brass-bound album with several plates of photographs.
- *length 23cm*
- £165   • Castlegate

Signed Gelatin Print ◀
- *1965*
"Ringo" by John "Hoppy"
Hopkins. Featuring John Lennon.
- *length 30cm*
- £350
- Photographers' Gallery

Signed C-Type ▲
- *1965*
"Hulme" by Shirley Baker.
- *length 40cm*
- £250
- Photographers' Gallery

C-Type Print ◀
- *20th century*
Signed recto by Julian Germain
from "Soccer Wonderland" series.
- *length 30cm*
- £300
- Photographers' Gallery

Colour Landscape ▼
- *20th century*
Untitled print from "Moving
Landscape"series by Chrystel Lebas.
Edition of ten, signed verso.
- £450
- Photographers' Gallery

Signed C-Type ▲
- *1998*
Signed limited edition of three,
"Lina", by Annelies Strbar.
- *length 17.5cm*
- £1,320
- Photographers' Gallery

Silver Gelatin Print ▲
- *20th century*
"Monsieur Plitt Teaching Tupy to
Jump over the Brook" by Jacques-
Henri Lartigue.
- *length 75cm*
- £1,850
- Photographers' Gallery

Signed Gelatin Print ▶
- *1958*
"Swimming Pool, Welch, West
Virginia" by O. Winston Link.
- *length 50cm*
- £1,350
- Photographers' Gallery

Cibachrome Print ∨
- *20th century*
Untitled from "The Wild West" series by David Levinthal. Edition limited to 25.
- *length 25cm*
- £500
- **Photographers' Gallery**

C-Type Print ➤
- *20th century*
Untitled girl in hammock photograph by Nat Finkelstein.
- *length 30cm*
- £550
- **Photographers' Gallery**

Estate Print ∧
- *20th century*
"Asleep on the job" by Weegee. Silver gelatin print.
- *length 27.5cm*
- £500
- **Photographers' Gallery**

Silver Gelatin Print ＜
- *1957*
"Vali Reflected in the Mirror" by Ed Van der Elsken.
- *length 42cm*
- £650
- **Photographers' Gallery**

Signed Gelatin Print ∨
- *1953*
"Nude, Eygalieres, France" by Bill Brandt. Signed recto.
- *length 50cm*
- £1,500
- **Photographers' Gallery**

Paris Print ∨
- *1951*
"Claudy and Vali in Claudy's Hotel Room" by Ed Van der Elsken.
- £2,050
- **Photographers' Gallery**

Photograph Album ＜
- *circa 1890*
Brass-mounted book with mother-of-pearl and rosewood inlay.
- *length 23cm*
- £295   • Castlegate

Shirley Baker Print ▼
- *1964*

"Salford, 1964" by Shirley Baker. A silver gelatin print, signed verso.
- *30.5cm x 35.5cm*
- £200 • Photo. Gallery

Silver Gelatin Print ▼
- *1955*

James Dean on the set of *Rebel Without a Cause* by photographer Bob Willoughby. Silver gelatin print, signed verso.
- *30.5cm x 40cm*
- £400 • Photo. Gallery

Matthew Murray Print ▼
- *1999*

"Morris Dancers, 1999" by Matthew Murray. C-Type print, signed verso.
- *30.5cm x 35.5cm*
- £200 • Photo. Gallery

Signed Willoughby Print ➤
- *1962*

"Billie Holliday, Tiffany Club, 1962" by Bob Willoughby. A silver gelatin print, signed verso.
- *30.5cm x 35.5cm*
- £400 • Photo. Gallery

Signed C-Type Print ▲
- *1952*

Marilyn Monroe photographed in 1952 by Bob Willoughby. C-Type print, signed verso.
- *30.5cm x 40cm*
- £600 • Photo. Gallery

Lartique Print ▼
- *1931*

"Cours automobile à Monthery, 1931" by Jacques-Henri Lartique. A silver gelatin print, signed verso.
- *30.5cm x 35.5cm*
- £2,800 • Photo. Gallery

Bob Willoughby Print ◄
- *1962*

"Audrey Hepburn, 1962" by Bob Willoughby. A silver gelatin print, signed verso.
- *25.5cm x 30.5cm*
- £600 • Photo. Gallery

Expert Tips

Pictures of famous people, from film stars to politicians, including those who have fallen from fame, often make a good investment. Fewer prints in circulation usually leads to an increase in their value.

Silver Gelatin Print ▲
- *1987*

"North Islands in dry docks, Smith's Dock 1987" by Ian Macdonald. Silver gelatin print, signed verso.
- *51cm x 35.5cm*
- £600 • Photo. Gallery

Expert Tips

Look out for prints that capture a freak or unusual moment, or that portray a familiar subject in surroundings that are out of context. Some photographs are now ranked alongside art so it is worth concentrating on collecting the work of a favourite up-and-coming photographer.

C-Type Print ▼
- *1999*

Untitled C-type print by photographer Nigel Shafran. Signed verso.
- *25.5cm x 35.5cm*
- £300 • Photo. Gallery

Untitled Print ▲
- *circa 1950*

Untitled silver gelatin print from the 1950s, signed recto by photographer Bert Hardy.
- *12cm x 16cm*
- £1,300 • Photo. Gallery

Ian Macdonald Print ▶
- *circa 1980*

Untitled silver gelatin print by photographer Ian Macdonald. Signed verso.
- *30.5cm x 40cm*
- £500 • Photo. Gallery

Signed C-Type Print ▼
- *2000*

"Kitchen Sink" by Nigel Shafran. C-type print, signed verso.
- *51cm x 35.5cm*
- £750 • Photo. Gallery

Untitled C-Type Print ▼
- *1998*

Untitled C-type print taken in 1998 by Jason Oddy, from the "Palace of Nations" series. Signed verso.
- *30.5cm x 35.5cm*
- £500 • Photo. Gallery

Signed Brandt Print ▼
- **1956**
"Nude, London, 1956" by Bill Brandt. A silver gelatin print, signed recto.
- *30.5cm x 40cm*
- **£1,800**   • Photo. Gallery

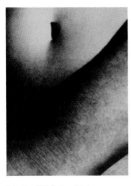

Limited Edition Print ▼
- **1965**
"Andy and Cow Wallpaper, 1965" by Nat Finkelstein. Silver gelatin print from an edition limited to 10. Signed verso.
- *30.5cm x 40cm*
- **£600**   • Photo. Gallery

Signed Silver Gelatin ▶
- *circa 1994*
"Milton Keynes" by Leo Regan. Silver gelatin print, signed verso
- *30.5cm x 40cm*
- **£300**   • Photo. Gallery

Bill Brandt Print ▲
- **1930**
"Parlour Maid at Window, Kensington, 1930" by Bill Brandt. Silver gelatin print, signed recto.
- *30.5cm x 40cm*
- **£1,300**   • Photo. Gallery

Silver Gelatin Print ◀
- **1937**
Signed silver gelatin print by Humphrey Spender of two small children playing on a wasteland in Bolton, Lancashire. For mass observation
- *30.5cm x 40cm*
- **£300**   • Photo. Gallery

Limited C-Type Print ▲
- **1965**
"Edie Sedgwick in Red Dress, 1965" by Nat Finkelstein. C-type print, from a limited edition of eight. Signed and numbered verso.
- *30.5cm x 40cm*
- **£650**   • Photo. Gallery

John Hopkins Print ⌃
- *1964*

"Thelonius Monk" taken in 1964 by John 'Hoppy' Hopkins. Silver gelatin print, signed recto.
- *30.5cm x 40cm*
- £350   • Photo. Gallery

Cornel Lucas Print ⌄
- *1948*

"Yvonne de Carlo as Salome" by Cornel Lucas. A silver gelatin print, signed recto and titled verso.
- *30.5cm x 40cm*
- £400   • Photo. Gallery

Silver Gelatin Print ⌃
- *1948*

"Movie cameraman in the South Pacific, 1948" by Cornel Lucas. Silver gelatin print, signed recto.
- *30.5cm x 40cm*
- £400   • Photo. Gallery

C-Type Print ⌃
- *2000*

"Hot Dandelion, 2000" by photographer Delilah Dyson. C-type print, signed verso.
- *30.5cm x 40cm*
- £250   • Photo. Gallery

Humphrey Spender Print ⌃
- *1937*

"Bolton, 1937" by Humphrey Spender. For mass observation. Silver gelatin print, signed and titled recto.
- *30.5cm x 40cm*
- £300   • Photo. Gallery

Signed Print ⌄
- *2000*

"Snow Drops, 2000" by Delilah Dyson. C-type print, signed verso.
- *30.5cm x 40cm*
- £300   • Photo. Gallery

Silver Gelatin Print ⌃
- *1955*

"The Popes and the last passenger steam train, 1955" taken by O. Winston Link.
Silver gelatin print, signed verso by the photographer.
- *30.5 x 40cm*
- £1,750   • Photo. Gallery

Posters

Jungle Book Poster ▲
- *circa 1967*
Released by Buena Vista with
credits to voice talents.
- *length 1m, width 69cm*
- £300 • **Reel Poster Gallery**

Andy Warhol's "Bad" ▲
- *circa 1977*
Artwork by John Van
Hamersveld. With caption.
- *length 1m, width 69cm*
- £325 • **Reel Poster Gallery**

2001: A Space Odyssey ▼
- *circa 1968*
Entitled "The Ultimate Trip" and
signed by Kaplan.
- *length 1m, width 69cm*
- £3,000 • **Reel Poster Gallery**

Coca-Cola Card Sign ▼
- *circa 1940*
A Coca-Cola card sign with
caption "Have a Coke".
- *height 65cm*
- £115 • **Dodo**

Stand-Up Card Sign ➤
- *circa 1940*
A Hartley's three-dimensional
stand-up card sign.
- *height 53cm*
- £160 • **Dodo**

Goldfinger Poster ▲
- *circa 1964*
Original French poster by Jeism
Mascii. Released by United
Artists. Captions in French.
- *length 79cm, width 61cm*
- £500 • **Reel Poster Gallery**

Anatomy of Murder ▲
- *circa 1959*
Graphic artist style by Saul Bass.
Photographs by Sam Leavitt.
- *length 1m, width 76cm*
- £850 • **Reel Poster Gallery**

Card Sign ➤
- *circa 1900*
A Kenyon & Craven's card sign advertising jams and marmalade.
- *height 40cm*
- £245
- Dodo

Curse of Frankenstein ▲
- *circa 1957*
Japanese, paper-backed and signed by Christopher Lee.
- *length 76cm, width 51cm*
- £950 • Reel Poster Gallery

Embossed Tin Sign ▲
- *circa 1910*
An embossed tin sign showing an advertisement for alcohol.
- *height 31cm*
- £175 • Dodo

Showcard ▼
- *circa 1950*
A showcard advertising Twinsol pure wool socks.
- *height 65cm*
- £20 • Radio Days

Un Homme et une Femme ▼
- *circa 1966*
A montage of photo images from the film, in Eastman colours.
- *length 79cm, width 61cm*
- £1,250 • Reel Poster Gallery

Star Wars Poster ▲
- *circa 1977*
With Polish translation and paper-backed. Artwork by Jakub Enol.
- *length 97cm, width 69cm*
- £425 • Reel Poster Gallery

Pseudonym Autonym ▲
- *circa 1890*
An Aubrey Beardsley original poster. English but printed in France.
- *length 50cm*
- £380 • Victor Arwas

Get Carter ▼
- *circa 1971*
With photographic captions from
the film by M.G.M.
- *length 1m, width 69cm*
- £425 • Reel Poster Gallery

"Reine de Joie" Poster ▼
- *circa 1890*
An original poster showing a
large man with a lady in a red
dress on his lap.
- *length 30cm*
- £800 • Victor Arnas

Le Mans ▲
- *circa 1971*
French poster showing Steve
McQueen. Artist Rene Fenacci.
- *length 61cm, width 41cm*
- £150 • Reel Poster Gallery

Jess II Bandito ▲
- *circa 1939*
Showing actor Tyrone Power.
Released by 20th Century Fox.
- *length 2m, width 1.4m*
- £1,800 • Reel Poster Gallery

Sleeping Beauty ▼
- *circa 1959*
A paper-backed poster of Walt
Disney's *Sleeping Beauty* showing
various characters from the story
and the title "Awaken to a World
of Wonders!".
- *length 76cm, width 51cm*
- £300 • Reel Poster Gallery

Planet of the Apes ▼
- *circa 1968*
A linen-backed, cartoon style
Romanian poster with title
"Planeta Maimutelor".
- *length 97cm, width 69cm*
- £950 • Reel Poster Gallery

Psycho ◄
- *circa 1960*
Showing Alfred Hitchcock on a
blank background. Printed in
England by W. E. Berry and
released by Paramount Pictures.
In style B.
- *length 1m, width 76cm*
- £5,000 • Reel Poster Gallery

Gimme Shelter ▼
- 1970
Original US poster, paper backed, for the Rolling Stones' film *Gimme Shelter*.
- 104cm x 69cm
- £350   • Reel Poster Gallery

Rebellion/Bunt ▶
- 1967
Original Polish poster, paper backed, featuring artwork by Rapnicki.
- 84cm x 58cm
- £150   • Reel Poster Gallery

Jour de Fête ◀
- 1948
Original French poster, linen backed, for the Jacques Tati film *Jour de Fête*, featuring artwork by Eric.
- 160cm x 119cm
- £2,500
- Reel Poster Gallery

Przygoda L'Avventura ▲
- 1959
Original Polish poster, paper backed, by Jan Lenica.
- 84cm x 58cm
- £250   • Reel Poster Gallery

Viaggio in Italia ▲
- 1953
Original Italian poster, linen backed, by Mauro Innocenti for the film *Viaggio in Italia*.
- 201cm x 140cm
- £1,800 • Reel Poster Gallery

Que Viva Mexico ◀
- 1932
Original east German poster, paper backed, by Wenzer.
- 81cm x 58cm
- £180   • Reel Poster Gallery

F for Fake ▼
- 1973

Original US poster, linen backed, designed by Donn Trethewey.
- 104cm x 69cm
- £500 • Reel Poster Gallery

The Graduate ▼
- 1967

Original US poster, linen backed, designed by United Artists Corporation.
- 206cm x 104cm
- £2,250 • Reel Poster Gallery

Turtle Diary ➤
- 1985

Original British poster, paper backed, featuring artwork by Andy Warhol, for the film *Turtle Diary*.
- 76cm x 102cm
- £225 • Reel Poster Gallery

Les Diaboliques ▲
- 1955

Original French poster, linen backed, style A, with artwork by Raymondgid.
- 160cm x 119cm
- £1,500 • Reel Poster Gallery

La Donna Che Visse due Volte/Vertigo ▲
- 1958

Original Italian poster featuring art by Sandro Simeoni, for the Hitchcock film *Vertigo*.
- 140cm x 99cm
- £1500 • Reel Poster Gallery

Expert Tips

The condition and rarity of a poster enhance its value, so focus on these factors. Film posters distributed and printed in small countries have become rare and are a good investment.

Sueurs Froides/ Cold Sweat ◄
- 1958

Original French poster, paper backed, art by Claude Venin.
- 79cm x 61cm
- £425 • Reel Poster Gallery

Radio, TV & Sound Equipment

Bendix Model 526C ▼
- **1946**
Black Bakelite American radio with the inscription "Strong Machine Age".
- *28cm x 35cm*
- **£750**
- **Decodence**

Fada Streamliner ▲
- **1940**
American onyx and amber streamlined Catalin radio, with large oval dial on the right.
- *height 19cm*
- **£1,000**
- **Decodence**

GEC Radio ▼
- *circa 1950*
GEC radio with Bakelite handles.
- *32cm x 44cm x 17cm*
- **£55**
- **Radio Days**

Intercom Speaker ◄
- **1940s**
English Art Deco-style red intercom system speaker, tube operated.
- *height 28cm*
- **£100**
- **Decodence**

Sonorette ▲
- **1940s**
French brown radio in bakelite, with a bulbous form and grille-design speaker.
- *height 34cm*
- **£500**
- **Decodence**

Emersa Radio ▲
- **1932**
American Art Deco Bakelite radio with a central fan design.
- *40cm x 50cm*
- **£300**
- **Decodence**

Ekco Table Model ▲

- *circa 1939*
Model TA201. Original price 22
guineas. Vision only (sound was
obtained by tuning a suitable
radio to the TV channel).
- *height 50cm*
- **£600**　　• **Vintage Wireless**

"KB" Wooden Radio ▲

- *circa 1940*
Fully working radio. One of many
produced in Great Britain during
the Second World War.
- *height 46cm*
- *width 53cm*
- **£125**　　• **Radio Days**

Bush TV ▼

- *circa 1949*
22 Model. Most desired of all
British Bakelite TVs.
- *height 39cm*
- **£300**　　• **Decodence**

TV/Radio & Gramophone ▼

- *1938*
R.G.D. (Radio Gramophone
Developments) model RG. Top of
the range radiogram. Image
viewed through mirror in the lid.
- *height 92.5cm*
- **£3,250**　　• **Vintage Wireless**

CKCO Model AD75 ▲

- *circa 1940*
Wartime English bakelite radio
designed by Wells Coates to meet
marine needs.
- *height 35cm*
- **£700**　　• **Decodence**

Expert Tips

*The Second World War was the
golden age of radio production
in the UK. The government
needed the medium for morale
purposes and insisted on
economical manufacture.*

Marconi Mastergram ▼

- *1937*
Model 703 TV/radio/auto-
radiogram. Same chassis as HMV
equivalent and originally costing
120 guineas.
- *height 97.5cm*
- **£3,000**　　• **Vintage Wireless**

Silver Tone Bullet 6110 ◄

- *circa 1938*
Modern design push-button radio
with enormous rotating turning
scale. Designed by Clarence
Karstacht.
- *height 17cm*
- **£1,100**　　• **Decodence**

Invicta Table Model ▼
- *date 1939*
Model TL5, made by Pye of
Cambridge. This is the only
known model of Invicta.
- *height 47.5cm*
- £800 ● Vintage Wireless

Philips Radio ▼
- *circa 1931*
Hexagonal with oxidised bronze
grill. Sought after for its unusual
appearance.
- *height 43cm*
- £500 ● Decodence

Crystal Set ▲
- *circa 1910*
An English Edwardian crystal set
in mahogany case with brass
fittings. In good condition.
- *height 30cm*
- £585 ● TalkMach

Grille Radio ▲
- *circa 1945*
Chunky automobile fender grille
radio. Made by Sentinel. Very
desirable.
- *height 19cm*
- £1,000 ● Decodence

JVC Television ▼
- *circa 1968*
A JVC "Space Helmet" television
of spherical form on a square
plinth. Monochrome reception.
- *height 60cm*
- £200 ● TalkMach

Portable Radio ▼
- *circa 1955*
A small portable radio with
original leather protective case.
Medium and long waves.
- *height 11cm*
- £45 ● TalkMach

Expert Tips

*Most radios need to be in full
working order; if they are not,
then they need to be remarkably
unusual or celebrity-connected
to be collectable.*

Mains Radio ▶
- *circa 1950*
A very small, red-cased mains
radio by Packard Bell of the
U.S.A., with large central dial
and minimal controls.
- *height 14cm*
- £140 ● TalkMach

Rock & Pop

Manic Street Preachers Single ▲
- 1990
"UK Channel Boredom" flexi-disc supplied with both fanzines.
- 18cm x 18cm
- £120   • Music & Video

Powder Compact ▲
- circa 1963
Circular powder compact featuring a Dezo Hoffman black and white shot of The Beatles.
- £475   • More Than Music

Madonna Lucky Star Single ▲
- 1983
Full-length version of the single "Lucky Star" by Madonna.
- 30cm x 30cm
- £80   • Music & Video

Strawbs with Sandy Denny Album ▼
- 1969
Strawbs music sampler No. 1, issued as a limited edition of 100.
- 30cm x 30cm
- £675   • Music & Video

U2 Single ▼
- 1979
U2's first single "Three", individually numbered.
- 20cm x 30cm
- £350   • Music & Video

U2 Helmet ▼
- 1998
U2 helmet issued to promote the Best of 1980–1990 album. Limited edition of 50 units.
- 30cm x 25cm x 23cm
- £250   • Music & Video

Rolling Stones Album ▲
- 1971
Export edition of Rolling Stones Stone Age album.
- 30cm x 30cm
- £700   • Music & Video

At Home With Screamin' Jay Hawkins ➤

- *circa 1958*
Album by the late Jay Hawkins – known for the epic single "I Put a Spell on You".
- **£499**   • **Music & Video**

Beatles Parlophone A Label Demo ▲

- *1967*
A green A Label demo disc, featuring "Hello Goodbye" and "I am the Walrus".
- **£800**   • **More Than Music**

Mojo Magazine ▲

- *circa 1995*
Issue no. 24 showing The Beatles. Published in three colours – this one with a red background.
- **£20**
- **Book & Comic Exchange**

John Lennon Mug ▲

- *circa 1987*
One of a limited edition of 1,000 Royal Doulton mugs, modelled by Stanley James Taylor.
- **£750**   • **More Than Music**

Wings Album ◄

- *circa 1979*
Back to the Egg promo. Only picture disc manufactured for the MPL Christmas Party 1979.
- **£1,250**   • **Music & Video**

Tote Bag with Five 12-inch Singles ▲

- *1985*
Duran Duran tote bag containing five maxi 12-inch singles.
- *30cm x 35cm*
- **£75**   • **Music & Video**

Rolling Stones Album ◄

- *1975*
Japanese five LP, 62-track promo of *The Great History of The Rolling Stones*. Box comes with large book and OBI. Individually printed inner sleeves.
- **£347**   • **Music & Video**

Expert Tips

The most desirable objects are personal items belonging to the stars – such as clothes and instruments – preferably accompanied by a photograph of the star using or wearing them.

Knebworth Park ▲
- **date 5th July 1974**
Official programme for Pink
Floyd's open-air concert at
Knebworth Park.
- **£65**   • **Music & Video**

John's Children ▲
- **circa 1967**
Copy of *Desdemona* by John's
Children, featuring Marc Bolam
and banned by the BBC.
- **£100**   • **Music & Video**

Iron Maiden Picture Disc ▼
- **circa 1983**
A picture disc of Iron Maiden's
Peace of Mind album, illustrated
on both sides.
- **£40**   • **Music & Video**

The Verve ▼
- **circa 1992**
Mint condition copy of *Voyager 1*,
recorded live in New York, by
The Verve.
- **£65**   • **Music & Video**

Mojo ▲
- **circa 1995**
Mojo issue no. 24 showing The
Beatles. Published with three
different covers, this one with a
blue background.
- **£20**
- **Book & Comic Exchange**

Expert Tips

*Brian Epstein, The Beatles'
manager, was famously dismissive
of the value of merchandising. As
a result, "official" souvenirs
proliferate and prices are
unpredictable.*

Beatles Sketch ▼
- **circa 1967**
An original sketch of Paul
McCartney from The Beatles'
film *Yellow Submarine*.
- **£300**   • **Music & Video**

Elvis 68 ◄
- **circa 1988**
A copy of the NBC TV
'Comeback Special'
commemorative Elvis Presley
promotional album.
- **£125**   • **Music & Video**

Beatles Archive Footage ◄
- *1964*

Two four-minute standard 8, silent, black and white reels. Of *London and Kennedy Airports* and *The Beatles Triumphant Appearance in the U.S.A.* In original box.
- **£195 each**
- **More Than Music**

Beatles Dress ▲
- *circa 1964*

Official Dutch Beatles' cotton dress in mustard with polka dots. With the makers' card tag.
- **£395** • **More Than Music**

Portrait by Joe Meek ▲
- *circa 1966*

"Pat as I see Him" – pen and ink on envelope by producer Joe Meek of his boyfriend.
- **£5,950** • **Music & Video**

Untied Diaries Box Set ▼
- *1988*

Untied Diaries edition 30, with 32 cassettes individually recorded and packaged. This is different from the vinyl version.
- **£900** • **Music & Video**

Heavy Metal ▼
- *circa 1977*

Issue no. 1 of *Heavy Metal* magazine, pursuivant on the cult film of the same name.
- **£20**
- **Book & Comic Exchange**

Beatles Talc Powder ▲
- *1964*

Talcum powder tin with different studies of the loveable mop-tops on either side. By Margo of Mayfair.
- *height 18cm*
- **£450** • **More Than Music**

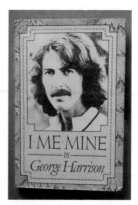

Harrison Autobiography ▲
- *1980*

Rare, unsigned hardback copy of first edition of Beatle George Harrison's autobiography *I Me Mine*, with dust cover. Published by Simon Schuster.
- **£75** • **More Than Music**

Official Carded Beatles Accessories ➤
- 1964
Sales cards containing Beatles cufflinks and tie-pin, with the group's heads cast in brass.
- £245 (left), £175 (right)
- More Than Music

The Who Album ▼
- 1965
The Who's *My Generation* album, by Brunswick, with original band line-up on cover. Poor condition.
- £40   • Music & Video

Official Carded Jewellery Box ◄
- 1964
Oval leather and brass accessories, with The Beatles' faces featured on the lid of the box.
- £225   • More Than Music

Official Corgi Toy ▲
- 1968
Die-cast metal yellow submarine with revolving periscope and one yellow and one white hatch. From the movie.
- £375   • More Than Music

Official Brooch ▲
- 1964
Official Nicki Byrne-designed Beatles brooch, with guitar and drum interwoven with the group's name and ceramic plaque showing their image, all on the original sales card.
- £250   • More Than Music

Expert Tips

There was much more scope for worthwhile artwork on the vinyl album covers of the 60s and 70s than on the subsequent cassette and compact disk covers. This is reflected in the prices of original artwork of the period.

Beatles Sneakers ◄
- circa 1964
Official "Wing Dings" Beatles sneakers, with images and signatures of the group on the shoes and the original box. In excellent condition.
- £795   • More Than Music

Siouxsie and The Banshees Memorabilia ➤

- *1981*

Half-page artwork for promotion of the *Arabian Knights* tour by Siouxsie and the Banshees.
- *40cm x 35cm*
- £175   • Music & Video

Bruce Springsteen Single ▲

- *1981*

"Cadillac Ranch" single by Bruce Springsteen.
- *18cm x 18cm*
- £25   • Music & Video

Beach Boys Album ▲

- *circa 1966*

Special disc jockey/producer copy of *The Best of the Beach Boys* album, released by EMI Records, London.
- £184   • Music & Video

The Police Singles Box ▲

- *1990*

Embossed wooden box containing 10 gold vinyl singles together with a picture disc by The Police.
- *18cm x 18cm*
- £195   • Music & Video

Manic Street Preachers Single ◄

- *1988*

Double A-side single "Suicide Alley Tennessee" containing a letter from the band.
- *18cm x 18cm*
- £995   • Music & Video

Album Artwork ◄
● *1984*
Unused album artwork for
Jimmy the Hoover by Jamie Reid,
with glass broken and damaged
intentionally for the "Leaving the
21st Century" series held at the
Mayfair gallery.
● *50cm x 50cm*
● **£200**   ● **Music & Video**

4AD Calendar ▼
● *1993*
Collector's item calendar
issued by record company,
4AD, and designed
by 23 Envelope.
● *35cm x 55cm*
● **£25**   ● **Music & Video**

Brute Force Album featuring John Lennon ▼
● *1970*
Extemporaneous album
by Brute Force featuring John
Lennon.
● **£395**   ● **Music & Video**

Withdrawn Single ▼
● *1981*
"Ha ha I'm drowning" single by
The Teardrop Explodes.
Withdrawn issue.
● *18cm x 18cm*
● **£60**   ● **Music & Video**

Wing's Record Sleeve ▼
● *1975*
Record sleeve for Wing's "Listen
to what the man said" and "King
Alfred's Rubbish", autographed
by Paul and Linda McCartney.
● **£675**   ● **More Than Music**

Rolling Stones Album ▼
● *1971*
Copy of the Rolling Stones album
Sticky Fingers.
● *30cm x 30cm*
● **£240**   ● **Music & Video**

Scripophilly & Paper Money

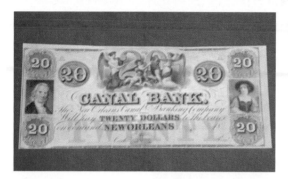

National Currency 20 Dollar Note ▼
- 1900
$20 note issued by the Citizen's Bank of Eureka, Kansas, during the Battle of Lexington.
- £595 • C. Narbeth

New Orleans Note ▲
- *circa 1860*
New Orleans $20 note issued by Canal Bank.
- £12.50 • C. Narbeth

Confederate States Note ▼
- 1864
Confederate States $10 note issued in the US Civil War.
- £28 • C. Narbeth

Military Payment Note ▼
- 1970
Military payment certificate to the value of 10 cents.
- £6 • C. Narbeth

Colonial Note ▶
- 1773
Colonial 15 shillings note issued in Pennsylvania. Numbered and signed by hand.
- £48 • C. Narbeth

American Note ▲
- 1995
American note to the amount of $2.
- £3 • C. Narbeth

500 Rouble Note ◄
- *1912*

A large Russian 500 rouble note, showing a portrait of Peter the Great. In extremely fine condition.
- £5   • C. Narbeth

Boer War Note ▼
- *1900*

A South African Boer War note of five pounds, issued from Pretoria, the Boer capital. In very fine condition.
- £28   • C. Narbeth

Hungarian Pengo Note ▲
- *1946*

100,000 billion pengo note – reflecting the world's highest ever inflation in post-war Hungary. In extremely fine condition.
- £3.50   • C. Narbeth

Three Pence Note ▲
- *circa 1960*

A British Armed Forces three pence note, mainly for use by the British Army of the Rhine in Germany.
- £12.50   • C. Narbeth

Letter from Edward VII ▼
- *18th January 1910*

A crested letter and photo regarding his private affairs. Addressed to his sister-in-law, the Duchess of Connaught,t and sent from Sandringham.
- £650   • Jim Hanson

Siege of Khartoum Note ▲
- *circa 1884*

A 20 piastre note from the siege of Khartoum, Sudan. Hand-signed by General Gordon and in very fine condition.
- £275   • C. Narbeth

Squad Photograph ▲
- *1966*

Signed, commemorative photograph of the England 1966 World Cup winning team, featuring Alf Ramsey, the team manager, Bobby Moore, the captain and players Nobby Stiles and Martin Peters, with signatures of the entire winning team. A full squad photograph is also included.
- £2,500   • Star Signings

Chinese Cash Note ▶
- *circa 1858*

A Chinese 2,000 cash note issued during the Taiping Rebellion. In very fine condition.
- £65   • C. Narbeth

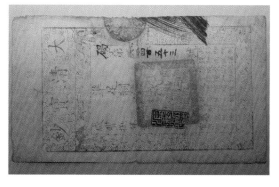

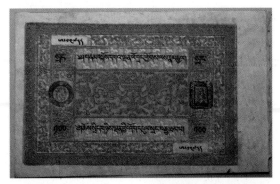

Tibetan Note ◀
- *circa 1950*

A 100 strang denomination note from Tibet, serial numbers applied by hand by Buddhist monks. One seal represents the monetary authority and the other that of the Dalai Lama. Uncirculated.
- £22   • C. Narbeth

Swedish Kronor ▲
- *1940*

A Swedish five kronor note. Extremely fine.
- £9.50   • C. Narbeth

African Republic Note ▲
- *circa 1974*

A 500 franc note from the Central African Republic, showing President Bokassa in a military pose. In mint condition.
- £70   • C. Narbeth

Letter from George V ▼
- *19th October 1873*

Written by the future king, then aged eight, from Marlborough House, to Lady Julia Lockwood.
- £650   • Jim Hanson

Austrian 1,000 Kronen ▲
- *1919*

An Austrian tausend Kronen note in mint condition.
- £3.50   • C. Narbeth

Five Reichsmark Note ▲
- *circa 1942*

Dated from the Second World War and showing a Hitler Youth in the Horst Wessel mould.
- £10   • C. Narbeth

Expert Tips

Check that the four corners of a note are sharp; hold it up to the light to check for creases; if it curls in the palm of the hand, it has been ironed.

Fifty Mark Note ▼
- *circa 1933*

A German 50 mark note. Extremely fine condition.
- £3.50   • C. Narbeth

Ugandan Bank Note ➤
- *circa 1973*

An Idi Amin Ugandan bank note of five shillings' value. Extremely fine note.
- £4.50   • C. Narbeth

Bank of England Note ▼
- *1972*

£20 note bearing a portrait of
Queen Elizabeth II.
- *£1972* • C. Narbeth

Fijiian Treasury Note ▲
- *12th July 1873*

Treasury note in the amount of
£50, issued in Fiji.
- *£495* • C. Narbeth

Railway Bond ◄
- *1911*

Bond issued by the Brazil Railway
Company.
- *£18* • C. Narbeth

US Railway Bond ▼
- *1881*

$500 dollar bond issued by the
Indiana Coal and Railway Co.
- *£35* • C. Narbeth

English Note ◄
- *1950*

White £5 note issued by the Bank
of England.
- *£89.50* • C. Narbeth

Railroad Shares ▲
- *1864*

Share issued by the Little Miami
Railroad Company.
- *£10* • C. Narbeth

English Banknote ▼
- *1987*

English £50 note signed by
David Somerset.
- *£95* • C. Narbeth

Signed US Share ▲
- *1895*

Philadelphia and Lancaster
share signed "Bingham". Early
US share with a vignette.
- *£795* • C. Narbeth

Russian Note ▲
- *1884*

Russian 10 rouble note issued in
the reign of Czar Alexander III.
- *£850* • C. Narbeth

Chinese Bond ➤
- **1911**
£20 bond issued by the Imperial Chinese Government.
- **£65**　　　　● C. Narbeth

Portuguese Bond ▲
- **1922**
Bond issued by the Companhia Colonial Navegaedo.
- **£7**　　　　● C. Narbeth

Iraqi Note ▼
- **1931**
ID 1 banknote, numbered A 157545, from Iraq.
- **£450**　　　　● C. Narbeth

Swiss Note ▲
- **1952**
SFr 5 note issued by the national bank of Switzerland.
- **£38**　　　　● C. Narbeth

British Linen Co. Note ▲
- **18th January 1896**
£5 note issued by the British Linen Company.
- **£325**　　　　● C. Narbeth

Expert Tips

The first European banknote was printed in Scandinavia in 1661. Since then a wealth of paper money has been issued. Keep your eyes on bank notes as they are likely to become a worthwhile investment.

Irish Banknote ▼
- **1977**
£50 note issued by The Central Bank of Ireland.
- **£175**　　　　● C. Narbeth

Bolivian Note ➤
- **1928**
$b1 note issued by the Central Bank of Bolivia.
- **£4**　　　　● C. Narbeth

Scottish Pound Note ▼
- **1969**
£1 note issued by the Bank of Scotland.
- **£25**　　　　● C. Narbeth

Sewing Items

Sewing Table ▼
- *circa 1840*

A lyre-ended chinoiserie sewing table of the 19th-century.
- *height 65cm*
- **£750** • **North West 8**

Needle Case ▼
- *circa 1890*

Ivory and mother-of-pearl needle case with hinged lid and silver cornucopia.
- *length 7.5cm*
- **£149** • **Fulham**

Regency Table Cabinet ▲
- *circa 1815*

Shaped late-Regency table cabinet in rosewood, with mother-of-pearl inlay and fitted sewing tray.
- *width 32.5cm*
- **£1,800** • **Hygra**

Tunbridge Ware ▲
- *circa 1800*

A turned and painted early Tunbridge-ware sewing companion.
- *height 6cm*
- **£450** • **Hygra**

Small Sewing Machine ▼
- *circa 1900*

An American "Little Comfort", handle-driven sewing machine.
- *height 17.5cm*
- **£350** • **TalkMach**

Work Table ▼
- *circa 1850*

Scandinavian birchwood work table. With turned, adjustable central column.
- *height 1.1m*
- **£995** • **Old Cinema**

Compartmentalised Thread Box ◄
- *circa 1810*

A straw-work thread box.
- *width 44cm*
- **£180** • **Hygra**

Sewing Box ▼
- *circa 1800*
Early 19th-century sewing box in
pollarded oak and rosewood inlay.
Retaining its original lift-out tray.
- *width 28cm*
- £480   • Hygra

Chinese Sewing Box ▼
- *circa 1820*
Sewing box in Chinese lacquer.
The box stands on four carved
wooden feet. Chinese-made for
export to England.
- *width 42.5cm*
- £1,200   • Hygra

Miniature Singer ➤
- *circa 1935*
A cast-iron Singer sewing
machine of the Art Deco period,
hand-driven and with a raised
action and bobbin board.
- *height 13cm*
- £400   • TalkMach

Necessaire ▲
- *circa 1780*
An 18th-century tortoiseshell
and silver necessaire.
- *height 7.5cm*
- £1,200   • Hygra

Expert Tips

*Thomas Saint patented the
world's first sewing machine in
1790, in England.*

Carpet Sticher ◀
- *19th century*
An American hand-powered
carpet stitcher made by the
Singer factory.
- *length 59cm*
- £285   • Mathews

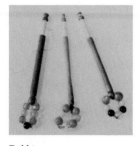

Bobbins ▲
- *circa 1930*
Selection of three fruitwood
bobbins with beaded decoration
and carved stems.
- *length 19cm*
- £4 each   • Mathews

Sewing Basket ▲
- *early 19th century*
A fine and delicate Anglo-Indian
sewing basket, with fretted ivory
panels framed with Sadeli mosaic.
- *width 20cm*
- £1,200   • Hygra

Hardwood Sewing Box

- *circa 1775*
An eighteenth-century sewing box with native and imported hardwoods juxtaposed and a neo-classical central motif.
- *width 29cm*
- £720   • Hygra

Kingwood Sewing Box   ▲

- *1830*
Kingwood sewing box inlaid with ivory in a diamond pattern, enclosing silver gilt needlework tools.
- *length 10cm*
- £490   • Thimble Society

Rosewood Sewing Box   ▲

- *circa 1835*
Fully fitted rosewood and mother-of-pearl sewing box labelled "George Johnston Glasgow".
- *width 31cm*
- £1,800   • Hygra

Inlaid Sewing Box   ▼

- *1820*
Very fine early nineteenth century Anglo-Indian ivory and sadeli mosaic fitted sewing box.
- *width 32cm*
- £950   • Hygra

Silver Thimbles   ▲

- *mid-19th century*
A selection of three silver thimbles with intricate silver skirts set with coloured stones.
- *height 2.6cm*
- £90 each   • Thimble Society

Sycamore Sewing Box   ▼

- *circa 1810*
A shaped sycamore fitted sewing box with a hand-painted design of a basket with overflowing flowers.
- *width 27cm*
- £1,800   • Hygra

Regency Sewing Box   ▼

- *1835*
Regency rosewood sewing box of sarcophagus form with pewter stringing, gadroon bordering, and lozenge feet. The interior with original red velvet and silk lining. The box contains a letter dated 1843, probably from the original owner.
- *16cm x 33cm x 26cm*
- £995   • J. & T. Stone

Snuff Boxes & Smoking Equipment

Spitfire Ashtray ▼
- *circa 1950*
Spitfire brass trophy ashtray.
On marble base. Spitfire with
pivot support.
- *height 15cm*
- £90   • Henry Gregory

Cigarette Box ▲
- *circa 1940*
Silver cigarette box with 18ct
gold sides. Smooth with a small
lip. By Boucheron, Paris.
- £2,000   • Henry Gregory

Monkey Snuff Box ▲
- *circa 1800*
Finely carved snuffbox in the
shape of a monkey.
- *height 7cm*
- £950   • A. & E. Foster

Horn Snuff Mull ▲
- *circa 1810*
Extremely rare silver-mounted
horn snuff mull. Made by Robert
Kaye of Perth, Scotland.
- *length 15cm*
- £1,750   • Nicholas Shaw

Match Strike ▼
- *circa 1900*
Glass circular match strike with
incised banding around outer
edge for striking.
- *height 12cm*
- £98   • Magpies

Goat Head Snuff Box ▲
- *late 19th century*
Snuff box in the shape of a goat's
head. Pewter fittings. Brown and
blue glaze with grey horns.
- *height 13cm*
- £1,100   • Elizabeth Bradwin

Expert Tips

*If a snuff box or similar item is
to be engraved, then it is best if
it is engraved in favour of a
famous person or event. Items
with re-engraving or erasing are
considered damaged.*

Wooden Snuffbox ▶
- *circa 1860*
Handcarved Scottish snuffbox.
- *length 6cm*
- *height 6cm*
- £1,250 • The Lacquer Chest

Cigar Cutter ▶
- *circa 1880*
Ivory and silver cigar cutter.
Monogrammed. No marks.
- *length 15cm*
- £420   • S. & A. Thompson

Gold and Tortoiseshell Snuff Box ➤

• 1702
Queen Anne gold and tortoiseshell snuff box made in London. The lid inset with a gold coin commemorating Queen Anne's coronation. One of 750 that were issued at the time.
• *length 8cm*
• £4,250   • N. Shaw

Silver Vesta Case ➤

• 1926
A silver George V vesta case made in London by The Goldsmith and Silversmith Company Ltd.
• *length 3cm*
• £675   • N. Shaw

Novelty Vesta Case ▲

• 1888
A silver Victorian novelty vesta case.
• *length 6cm*
• £575   • N. Shaw

Austrian Snuff Box ▼

• 1924
An Austrian snuff box with indigo enamel on a tooled silver base, with pierced floral cartouches in a neo-classical style.
• *length 8cm*
• £480   • Thimble Society

Silver Gilt Snuff Box ▲

• 1855
A Victorian silver gilt snuff box presented to Captain H. G. Kennedy of the ship *Parker*. Made by Edward Smith in Birmingham
• *length 11cm*
• £2,250   • N. Shaw

Mahogany Snuff Box ▲

• 1860
Mahogany shoe inlaid with brass design and mother of pearl.
• *6cm x 9cm*
• £525   • Bill Chapman

Cigar Box ❯
- **1920**

Unusual burr walnut cigar and cigarette box with gilded handle and decoration. Two lighter drawers with match strikers.
- *width 24cm*
- **£495** • J. & T. Stone

Silver Taper ❮
- **1880**

A Victorian, silver vesta/ taper lighter made in London by Louis Dee.
- *length 11cm*
- **£650** • N. Shaw

Continental Vesta Case ▲
- *circa 1900*

A continental vesta case decorated with an enamel chestnut horse's head.
- *3cm*
- **£450** • N. Shaw

Victorian Snuff Box ▼
- **1840**

A silver Victorian snuff box with an oak leaf pattern, presented to Mr William McKelvic of Redruth.
- *length 3.5cm*
- **£2,750** • N. Shaw

George IV Snuff Box ▼
- **1822–23**

A George IV snuff box made in Birmingham by Joseph Willmore.
- *length 4cm*
- **£450** • N. Shaw

Double Snuff Box ❯
- **1858**

A George IV double Regi Mari snuff box inscribed, "London 1827, Tria Juncta In Uno. Presented by Lieut Col Caulfield and the Married Officers of the mess of the 33rd Roscommon Regiment, 17 March 1858". Engraved with a four-leaf clover.
- *length 6cm*
- **£3,950** • N. Shaw

Expert Tips

Cigarette boxes are extremely collectable, especially the examples from the Art Deco period. Their value also increases if they are made from gold or silver and carry a hallmark. When purchasing these items it is important that one bears in mind the craftsmanship and style of the piece. Early cigar cutters will always command a high price, and any snuff box with a zoographical theme is always worth buying.

Telephones

Series 700 Telephone ▲
- *circa 1967*
British Telecom, acrylic with
rotary dial, flexicord and handset
extension. Resprayed in silver.
- £85 • After Noah

Viscount Telephone ▼
- *circa 1986*
A British Telecom-supplied
telephone in burnt orange with
cream flexcord extension.
- £20 • Retro

Bakelite Telephone ▼
- *circa 1950*
A GPO model telephone cast in
bakelite with rotary dial.
- £125 • H. Hay

Swiss Telephone ▲
- *circa 1950*
A Swiss wall-mounted telephone
with bell-ring displayed to top
and hook connection.
- £100 • Decodence

Elvis Presley Telephone ▲
- *circa 1980*
"Jailhouse Rock" shown with
guitar and period clothes. Touch
tone handset.
- £99 • Telephone Lines

Danish Telephone ▲
- *circa 1935*
A Danish magneto telephone
based on an L.M. Ericsson design.
Can't be used on today's system.
- £270 • Old Telephone Co

Expert Tips

*Collectors should be careful to
keep old bakelite telephones out
of direct sunlight, the greatest
enemy of antiques. It fades
them irreversibly.*

Upright Dial Telephone ➤
- *circa 1908*
Made from 1908 by Telefon
Fabrik Automatic of
Copenhagen.
- £510 • Old Telephone Co

Betacom "Golphone" ➤
- *mid-1980*
Model GFI. Made in Hong Kong
with golf-bag handset and push
buttons, mute tone and redial.
- £18   • Retro

Expert Tips

*The best polish for use on
telephones is hard beeswax. The
advantage that this has over
silicone polishes is that the latter
tend to make phones slippery
and easy to drop.*

Belgian Wall Phone ➤
- *circa 1960*
A Belgian wall phone repainted
in red. Made in Antwerp by Bell
Telephones, a subsidiary of the
American Bell Telephones.
- £180   • Old Telephone Co

Danish Telephone ▼
- *circa 1930*
Telephone with dial and hand-
raised cradle, made in Denmark
for the Danish telephone
authority.
- £350   • Old Telephone Co

500 Series Telephone ◄
- *circa 1978*
Made by Northern Telecom,
Stromberg-Carlson. Originally
supplied for an American airforce
base but resold in 1994. Unused
and in original sealed box.
- £95   • Old Telephone Co

300 Series Telephone ▼
- *circa 1955*
A 300 series black bakelite office
telephone with original handset,
cord and draw.
- £230   • Old Telephone Co

Audioline 310 Telephone ▲
- *circa 1980*
Red Audioline 310, with
oversized keypad with numbers
also in red, push-button controls
and black flexicord extension.
- £30   • Retro

R2D2 Telephone ▲
- *circa 1980*
A telephone in the form of the
character R2D2, from the *Star
Wars* films. His head moves and
lifts up when the phone rings.
- £99   • Telephone Lines

Ivory Telephone ➤
- *circa 1930*
A GPO telephone in ivory, rare for the period. Shows all-metal rotary dial with original central label and number/letter display.
- £395　　　　　● H. Hay

Danish Telephone ▲
- *circa 1935*
A variation on the D30, with two exchange lines coming in. Supplied with a separate bell set.
- £420　　● Old Telephone Co

Desk Telephone ▲
- *circa 1960*
A Belgian desk telephone in black plastic, with black rotary dial and white base on rubber feet.
- £150　　● Old Telephone Co

Magneto Telephone ▼
- *circa 1925*
A classic design by L. M. Ericsson, Stockholm, made from around 1896. Also known as Eiffel Tower.
- £850　　● Old Telephone Co

300 Series Telephone ▲
- *circa 1954*
By Siemens Brothers, Woolwich. Rarest colour in this series. Used for shared or party lines.
- £600　　● Old Telephone Co

Darth Vader Telephone ◄
- *circa 1980*
Telephone in the form of Darth Vader, from *Star Wars*, with moving head.
- £99　　　● Telephone Lines

Expert Tips

Ascertain from the dealer, when effecting your purchase, whether the telephone you are buying can be used on a modern system and, if so, what conversion equipment is necessary.

Trimphone ◄
- *circa 1970*
Silver-painted British "Trimphone" made for the GPO, with push-button dialling. With distinctive ringing tone.
- £85　　　　● After Noah

Queen's Silver Jubilee ◀
● *circa 1977*
Very rare and limited edition,
unused with type 64d bell set.
Introduced to commemorate the
25th year of Elizabeth II's reign.
● £150   ● Old Telephone Co

Ericofon Telephone ◀
● *circa 1955*
Designed in 1953 by Ralph Lysell
and Hugo Blomberg. In white
and red with dial underneath.
● £70   ● Telephone Lines Ltd

Bakelite Pyramid Phone ▲
● *circa 1930*
Series 200 with chrome rotary
dial, cloth flex and address drawer.
● £295   ● After Noah

300 Series Telephone ▼
● *circa 1957*
A rare 328 telephone made by
Plessey, Ilford, Essex. With bell-
on and bell-off push buttons.
● £650   ● Old Telephone Co

Model 1000 ▲
● *circa 1962*
Made by GEC of Coventry and
was intended as a replacement for
the 300 series but not adopted.
● £160   ● Old Telephone Co

Candlestick Telephone ▲
● *circa 1927*
Type 150, in bakelite, featuring a
replacement microphone. Made
by Ibex Telephones.
● £460   ● Old Telephone Co

Expert Tips

*Telephones do not have to work
in order to be collectable. Very
early ones are intrinsically
valuable as are some of the
antiques of the future – early
mobiles and car-phones.*

Genie Telephone ▶
● *circa 1978*
BT special range, a much sought-
after designer telephone in white
with metal dial.
● £39   ● Telephone Lines Ltd

Black Plastic Telephone ▲
- **1960**
Black plastic telephone with
white letters and numbers, and
black flex.
- *13cm x 13cm x 21cm*
- **£55**   • Radio Days

Ericsson Telephone ▶
- *circa 1905*
A Swedish-made, Ericsson,
wooden wall-mounted phone
with bell-ring display to top.
- *69cm x 26cm*
- **£495**   • Telephone Lines

Series 300 Telephone ▼
- **1940s–1950s**
An English acrylic golden yellow
telephone with drawer for
addresses and integral bell.
- *19cm x 18cm*
- **£300**   • Decodence

Candlestick Telephone ▲
- **1916**
French candlestick telephone
with metal and chrome handset
and wooden candlestick base by
Grammont.
- *height 34cm*
- **£415**   • Telephone Lines

Desk Telephone ▲
- **1895**
A Dutch wooden desk phone
with rotary dial.
- *height 15cm*
- **£295**   • Telephone Lines

Expert Tips

*Even if a phone is termed a
novelty phone this does not
imply that it is of low worth.
Bear in mind that these will be
the collectables of the future and
will increase in value as the
years go by, just remember to
keep the original box!*

Walking Sticks

Wooden Cane ▲
- *circa 1890*
Gargoyle head on a gnarled
wooden cane.
- *92cm x 6cm x 3cm*
- £240   • Henry Gregory

Snakewood Walking Cane ▲
- *circa 1900*
An elegant, rare snakewood cane
with gold collar and looped
handle.
- *length 89cm*
- £550   • Michael German

Whalebone Cane ▼
- *circa 1840*
A fine whalebone cane with full
barley twist shaft. The whale
handle loop carved with a
serpent's head.
- *length 70cm*
- £1,600   • Michael German

City Walking Cane ▼
- *circa 1900*
Ebonised cane with gioche
enamel ball, gold band and
Austrian mark.
- *length 55cm*
- £750   • Michael German

Hoof Walking Stick ▲
- *circa 1880*
Carved horn hoof handle
mounted on unusual segmented
shaft formed from paper washers.
- *length 100cm/handle*
- £650   • Michael German

Japanese Walking Cane ▲
- *circa 1900*
Japanese bamboo cane inset with
ivory face and silver collar.
- *length 20cm*
- £680   • Michael German

Russian Walking Cane ▲
- *circa 1890*
Russian ebonised cane with an elaborately decorated silver handle with overlaid enamel Tau and Russian marks
- *length 90cm*
- £1,400 • Michael German

Expert Tips

Items related to personalities plus the Royal connection are especially popular. Walking sticks were a playground for the craftsman. Some were hollowed out and fitted with stem like decanters, others with swords, horse measuring sticks or even to conceal a gun. Perhaps those most sought after are those with beautifully carved ivory grips, or those with a zoographical theme.

Cricket Ball Walking Stick ▼
- *circa 1870*
Unusual folk art cane with hand holding cricket ball, carved shaft.
- *length 100cm*
- £480 • Michael German

Chinese Walking Cane ◄
- *circa 1880–90*
An ornate silver cane from China with a long silver handle chased with a dragon design.
- *length 100cm*
- £680 • Michael German

Carved Walking Stick ▼
- *circa 1860*
Folk art cane with deeply carved animals, trees and fruit, silver collar and rounded top.
- *length 92cm*
- £925 • Michael German

Elephant Walking Cane ▼
- *circa 1890*
Ebonised cane with an ivory baby elephant with glass eyes, in a seated position.
- *length 78cm*
- £1,200 • Michael German

There follows a list of antique dealers, many of whom have provided items in the main body of the book and all of whom will be happy to assist within their areas of expertise.

Abacus Antiques
(ref: Abacus)
Grays Antiques Market,
58 Davies Street, London W1Y 2LP
Tel: 020 7629 9681

Antiques.

After Noah
121 Upper Street,
London N1 8ED
Tel: 020 7359 4281
Fax: 020 7359 4281
www.afternoah.com

Antique furniture, linen and postcards.

After Noah (Kings Road)
(ref: After Noah (KR))
261 Kings Road,
London SW3 5EL
Tel: 020 7351 2610
Fax: 020 7351 2610
www.afternoah.com

Antique furniture, linen and postcards.

Albany Antiques
(ref: Albany)
8–10 London Road, Hindhead,
Surrey GU26 6AF
Tel: 01428 605 528
Fax: 01428 605 528

*Georgian furniture, eighteenth-century brass,
Victorian antiques, porcelain and statuary.*

Armoury of St James, The
(ref: The Armoury)
17 Piccadilly Arcade,
London SW1Y 6NH
Tel: 020 7493 5083
Fax: 020 7499 4422
www.armoury.co.uk/home

Royal memorabilia and model soldiers.

Victor Arwas Gallery
(ref: Arwas)
3 Clifford Street,
London W1X 1RA
Tel: 020 7734 3944
Fax: 020 7437 1859
www.victorarwas.com

*Art Nouveau and Art Deco, glass, ceramics,
bronzes, sculpture, furniture, jewellery, silver,
pewter, books and posters, from 1880–1940.
Paintings, watercolours and drawings, 1880 to date.
Original graphics, lithographs, etchings and woodcuts
from 1890 to date.*

Linda Bee
Grays in the Mews Antiques Market,
1–7 Davies Mews,
London W1Y 1AR
Tel: 020 7629 5921
Fax: 020 7629 5921

Vintage costume jewellery and fashion accessories.

Beverley
30 Church Street,
Marylebone,
London NW8 8EP
Tel: 020 7262 1576
Fax: 020 7262 1576

*English ceramics, glass, metal, wood, pottery,
collectables and decorative items from 1850–1950.*

Book and Comic Exchange
(ref: Book & Comic)
14 Pembridge Road,
London W11 3HL
Tel: 020 7229 8420
www.buy-sell-trade.co.uk

Modern first editions, cult books and comics.

Malcolm Bord Gold Coin Exchange
(ref: Malcolm Bord)
16 Charing Cross Road,
London WC2 0HR
Tel: 020 7836 0631/020 7240 0479/
020 7240 1920

*Dealing in all types of coin, medal and
bank note.*

Elizabeth Bradwin
75 Portobello Road,
London W11 2QB
Tel: 020 7221 1121
Fax: 020 8947 2629
www.elizabethbradwin.com

Animal subjects.

Bridge Bikes
137 Putney Bridge,
London SW15 2PA
Tel: 020 8870 3934

Bikes.

Jasmin Cameron
Antiquarias Antiques Market,
135 Kings Road,
London SW3 4PW
Tel: 020 7351 4154
Fax: 020 7351 4154

*Drinking glasses and decanters 1750–1910,
vintage fountain pens and writing materials.***C. A.
R. S. of Brighton**

(ref: C. A. R. S.)
4–4a Chapel Terrace Mews,
Kemp Town, Brighton BN2 1HU
Tel: 01273 622 722
Fax: 01273 601 960
www.carsofbrighton.co.uk

*Classic automobilia and regalia specialists, and
children's pedal cars.*

**Cartoon Gallery, The
(ref: Cartoon Gallery)**
39 Great Russell Street,
London WC1 3PH
Tel: 020 7636 1011
Fax: 020 7436 5053

Comics.

**Mia Cartwright Antiques
(ref: Mia Cartwright)**
20th C. Theatre Arcade,
291 Westbourne Grove (Sats),
London W11
Tel: 01273 579700

Bill Chapman
Shop No. 11, Bourbon/
Hanby Antique Centre,
151 Sydney Street,
London SW3 6NT
Tel: 020 7351 5387

Collectables.

**Chelsea Military Antiques
(ref: Chelsea (OMRS))**
Stands N13–14, Antiquarius,
131–141 Kings Road,
London SW3 4PW
Tel: 020 7352 0308
Fax: 020 7352 0308
www.chelseamilitaria.co.uk

*Pre-1945 militaria, edge weapons, medals including
British and foreign campaign/gallantry medals.*

**John Clay Antiques
(ref: John Clay)**
263 New Kings Road,
London SW6 4RB
Tel: 020 7731 5677

*Furniture, objets d'art, silver and clocks from the
eighteenth and nineteenth century.*

Cobwebs
73 Avery Hill Road, New Eltham,
London SE9 2BJ
Tel: 020 8850 5611

Furniture, general antiques and collectables.

**Garrick D. Coleman
(ref: G. D. Coleman)**
75 Portobello Road,
London W11 2QB
Tel: 020 7937 5524
Fax: 020 7937 5530
www.antiquechess.co.uk

Antiques, fine chess sets and glass paperweights.

**Rosemary Conquest
(ref: R. Conquest)**
4 Charlton Place,
London N1 8AJ
Tel: 020 7359 0616

*Continental and Dutch lighting, copper, brass and
decorative items.*

**Curios Gardens & Interiors
(ref: Curios)**
130c Junction Road,
Tufnell Park,
London N19 5LB
Tel: 020 7272 5603
Fax: 020 7272 5603

*Garden furniture, statuary, reclaimed pine furniture
and antique furniture.*

Decodence
21 The Mall,
359 Upper Street,
London N1 0PD
Tel: 020 7354 4473
Fax: 020 7689 0680

Classic plastics such as bakelite, celluloid and catalin; vintage radios, lighting, telephones and toys.

Dodo
Stand Fo73, Alfie's Antiques Market,
13–25 Church Street,
London NW8 8DT
Tel: 020 7706 1545
Fax: 020 7724 0999

Posters, tins and advertising signs, 1890–1940.

Drummonds Architectural Antiques Ltd
(ref: Drummonds)
The Kirkpatrick Buildings,
25 London Road, Hindhead,
Surrey GU26 6AB
Tel: 01428 609444
Fax: 01428 609445
www.drummonds-arch.co.uk

Restored original and new bathrooms, reclaimed wood and stone flooring, fireplaces, statues, garden features, lighting, gates and railings, doors and door furniture, radiators, antique furniture, windows and large architectural features.

A. & E. Foster
Little Heysham, Forge Road, Naphill,
Buckinghamshire HP14 4SU
Tel: 01494 562024
Fax: 01494 562024

Antique treen works of art and early treen.

Fulham Antiques
(ref: Fulham)
320 Munster Road,
London SW6 6BH
Tel: 020 7610 3644
Fax: 020 7610 3644

Antique and decorative furniture, lighting and mirrors.

G Whizz
17 Jerdan Place,
London SW6 1BE
Tel: 020 7386 5020
Fax: 020 8741 0062
www.metrocycle.co.uk

Bikes.

Michael German Antiques
(ref: Michael German)
38b Kensington Church Street,
London W8 4BX
Tel: 020 7937 2771
Fax: 020 7937 8566
www.antiquecanes.com
www.antiqueweapons.com

Antique walking canes, antique arms and armour.

Gabrielle de Giles
The Barn at Bilsington,
Swanton Lane, Bilsington,
Ashford, Kent TN25 7JR
Tel: 01233 720917
Fax: 01233 720156

Antique and country furniture, home interiors, designer for curtains and screens.

Gosh
39 Great Russell Street,
London WC1B 3PH
Tel: 020 7436 5053
Fax: 020 7436 5053

Henry Gregory
82 Portobello Road,
London W11 2QD
Tel: 020 7792 9221
Fax: 020 7792 9221

Silver-plate, silver, sporting goods and decorative antiques.

Jim Hanson & Argyll Etkin Ltd
18 Claremont Field,
Ottery St Mary,
Devon EX11 1NP
Tel: 01404 815010
Fax: 01404 815224

Philatelist and postal historian.

Keith Harding's World of Mechanical Music
(ref: Keith Harding)
The Oak House,
High Street, Northleach,
Gloucestershire GL54 3ET
Tel: 01451 860181
Fax: 01451 861133
www.mechanicalmusic.co.uk

Gerard Hawthorn Ltd
(ref: Gerard Hawthorn)
104 Mount Street,
London W1Y 5HE
Tel: 020 7409 2888
Fax: 020 7409 2777

Chinese, Japanese and Korean ceramics and works of art.

Henry Hay
Unit 5054, 2nd floor,
Alfie's Market, 13–25 Church Street,
London NW8
Tel: 020 7723 2548

Art Deco and twentieth-century chrome and brass lamps and bakelite telephones.

Holland & Holland
31–33 Bruton Street,
London W1X 8JS
Tel: 020 7499 4411
Fax: 020 7409 3283

Guns.

Hope & Glory
131a Kensington Church Street
(entrance in Peel Street),
London W8 7LP
Tel: 020 7727 8424

Commemorative ceramics including royal and political subjects.

Jonathan Horne
66c Kensington Church Street,
London W8 4BY
Tel: 020 7221 5658
Fax: 020 7792 3090
www.jonathanhorne.co.uk

Early English pottery, medieval to 1820.

Huxtable's Old Advertising
(ref: Huxtable's)
Alfie's Market,
13–25 Church Street,
London NW8 8DT
Tel: 020 7724 2200

Advertising, collectables, tins, signs, bottles, commemoratives and old packaging from late Victorian.

Jessop Classic Photographica
(ref: Jessop Classic)
67 Great Russell Street,
London WC1
Tel: 020 7831 3640
Fax: 020 7831 3956

Classic photographic equipment, cameras and optical toys.

Kitchen Bygones
13–15 Church Street,
Marylebone,
London NW8 8DT
Tel: 020 7258 3405
Fax: 020 7724 0999

Kitchenalia.

Lacquer Chest, The
(ref: Lacquer Chest)
75 Kensington Church Street,
London W8 4BG
Tel: 020 7937 1306
Fax: 020 7376 0223

Military chests, china, clocks, samplers and lamps.

Langfords Marine Antiques
(ref: Langfords Marine)
The Plaza, 535 Kings Road,
London SW10 0SZ
Tel: 020 7351 4881
Fax: 020 7352 0763
www.langfords.co.uk

Nautical artefacts.

London Antique Gallery
(ref: London Antique)
66e Kensington Church Street,
London W8 4BY
Tel: 020 7229 2934
Fax: 020 7229 2934

Meissen, Dresden, Worcester, Minton, Shelley, Sèvrea, Lalique and bisque dolls.

Mac's Cameras
(ref: Mac's)
262 King Street, Hammersmith,
London W6 0SJ
Tel: 020 8846 9853

Antique camera equipment.

Magpies
152 Wandsworth Bridge Road,
London SW6 2UH
Tel: 020 7736 3738

Small furniture, kitchenware, door furniture, cutlery, lighting, silver and silver-plate.

A. P. Mathews
283 Westbourne Grove,
London W11
Tel: 01622 812590

Antique luggage.

More Than Music Collectables
(ref: More Than Music)
C24–25 Grays Mews Antiques Market,
1–7 Davies Mews,
London W1Y 2LP
Tel: 020 7629 7703
Fax: 01519 565510
www.mtmglobal.com

Rock and popular music memorabilia, specialising in The Beatles.

Murray Cards (International) Ltd
(ref: Murray Cards)
51 Watford Way,
London NW4 3JH
Tel: 020 8202 5688
Fax: 020 8203 7878
www.murraycards.com

Cigarette and trade cards

Music & Video Exchange
(ref: Music & Video)
38 Notting Hill Gate,
London W11 3HX
Tel: 020 7243 8574
www.mveshops.co.uk

CDs, memorabilia, vinyl – deletions and rarities.

Myriad Antiques
(ref: Myriad)
131 Portland Road,
London W11 4LW
Tel: 020 7229 1709
Fax: 020 7221 3882

*French painted furniture, garden furniture, bamboo,
Victorian and Edwardian upholstered chairs, mirrors
and objets d'art.*

Colin Narbeth and Son
(ref: C. Narbeth)
20 Cecil Court,
London WC2N 4HE
Tel: 020 7379 6975
Fax: 0172 811244
www.colin-narbeth.com

*Banknotes, bonds and shares of all countries and
periods.*

North West Eight
(ref: North West 8)
36 Church Street,
London NW8 8EP
Tel: 020 7723 9337

Decorative antiques.

Old School
130c Junction Road,
Tufnell Park,
London N19
Tel: 020 7272 5603

Gardens and interiors.

Old Telephone Company, The
(ref: Old Telephone Co.)
The Battlesbridge Antiques Centre,
The Old Granary, Battlesbridge,
Essex SS11 7RE
Tel: 01245 400 601
www.theoldtelephone.co.uk
Antique and collectable telephones.

Pendulum of Mayfair
King House, 51 Maddox Street,
London W1R 9LA
Tel: 020 7629 6606
Fax: 020 7629 6616

*Clocks: including longcase, bracket and wall,
and Georgian period furniture.*

Photographer's Gallery, The
(ref: Photo. Gallery)
5 Great Newport Street,
London WC2H 7HY
Tel: 020 7831 1772
Fax: 020 7836 9704
www.photonet.org.uk

Radio Days
87 Lower Marsh,
London SE1 7AB
Tel: 020 7928 0800
Fax: 020 7928 0800

*Lighting, telephones, radios, clothing, magazines and
cocktail bars from the 1930s–1970s.*

Ranby Hall Antiques
(ref: Ranby Hall)
Barnby Moor, Retford,
Nottingham DN22 8JQ
Tel: 01777 860696
Fax: 01777 701317
www.ranbyhall.antiques-gb.com

*Antiques, decorative items and contemporary
objects.*

Reel Poster Gallery
(ref: Reel Poster)
72 Westbourne Grove,
London W2 5SH
Tel: 020 7727 4488
Fax: 020 7727 4499
www.reelposter.com

Original vintage film posters.

Reel Thing, The
(ref: Reel Thing)
17 Royal Opera Arcade, Pall Mall,
London SW1Y 4UY
Tel: 020 7976 1830
Fax: 020 7976 1850
www.reelthing.co.uk

Purveyors of vintage sporting memorabilia.

Retro Exchange
20 Pembridge Road,
London W11
Tel: 020 7221 2055
Fax: 020 7727 4185
www.I/fel.trade.co.uk

Space age-style furniture and 1950's kitsch.

Retro Home
20 Pembridge Road,
London W11
Tel: 020 7221 2055
Fax: 020 7727 4185
www.I/fel.trade.co.uk

Bric-a-brac, antique furniture and objects of desire.

Shahdad Antiques
(ref: Shahdad)
A16–17 Grays-in-Mews,
1–7 Davies Mews,
London W1Y 2LP
Tel: 020 7499 0572
Fax: 020 7629 2176

Islamic and ancient works of art.

Nicholas Shaw Antiques
(ref: N. Shaw)
Great Grooms Antique Centre,
Parbrook, Billinghurst,
West Sussex RH14 9EU
Tel: 01403 786 656
Fax: 01403 786 656
www.nicholas-shaw.com

Scottish and Irish fine silver, small silver and collector's items.

Star Signings
Unit A18–A19 Grays Mews Antiques Market,
1–7 Davies Mews
London W1Y 2LP
Tel: 020 7491 1010
Fax: 020 7491 1070

Sporting autographs and memorabilia.

June & Tony Stone
(ref: J. & T. Stone)
75 Portobello Road,
London W11 2QB
Tel: 020 7221 1121

Fine antique boxes.

Talking Machine, The
30 Watford Way,
London NW4 3AL
Tel: 020 8202 3473
www.gramophones.endirect.co.uk

Mechanical antiques typewriters, radios, music boxes, photographs, sewing machines, juke boxes, calculators and televisions.

Telephone Lines Ltd
(ref: Telephone Lines)
304 High Street, Cheltenham,
Gloucestershire GL50 3JF
Tel: 01242 583699
Fax: 01242 690033
Telephones.

Thimble Society, The
(ref: Thimble Society)
Geoffrey van Arcade, 107 Portobello Road,
London W11 2QB
Tel: 020 7419 9562

Thimbles, sewing items, snuff boxes and lady's accessories.

Sue & Alan Thompson
(ref: S. & A. Thompson)
Highland Cottage, Broomne Hall Road,
Cold Harbour RH5 6HH
Tel: 01306 711970
Fax: 01306 711970

Objects of vertu, antique tortoiseshell items, period furniture and unusual collector's items.

Tredantiques
77 Hill Barton Road, Whipton,
Exeter EX1 3PW
Tel: 01392 447082
Fax: 01392 462200

Furniture.

Trio/Teresa Clayton
(ref: Trio)
L24 Grays Mews Antiques Market,
1–7 Davies Mews,
London W1Y 2LP
Tel: 020 7493 2736
Fax: 020 7493 9344

Perfume bottles and Bohemian glass.

Vintage Wireless Shop
(ref: Vintage Wireless)
The Hewarths Sandiacre,
Nottingham NG10 5NQ
Tel: 0115 939 3139

Radios.

Youll's Antiques
27–28 Charnham Street, Hungerford,
Berkshire RG17 0EJ
Tel: 01488 682046
Fax: 01488 684335
www.youll.com

English/French furniture from seventeenth to twentieth century, porcelain, silver and decorative items.

Index

Notes

Notes

MEASUREMENT CONVERSION CHART

This chart provides a scale of measurements converted from centimetres and metres to feet and inches.

1cm	$\frac{2}{5}$in
2cm	$\frac{4}{5}$in
3cm	$1\frac{1}{10}$in
4cm	$1\frac{3}{5}$in
5cm	2in
10cm	$3\frac{7}{8}$in
15cm	$5\frac{9}{10}$in
20cm	$7\frac{3}{4}$in
25cm	$9\frac{4}{5}$in
30cm	$11\frac{4}{5}$in
40cm	1ft $3\frac{3}{4}$in
50cm	1ft $7\frac{2}{3}$in
75cm	2ft $5\frac{1}{2}$in
1 m	3ft $3\frac{1}{3}$in
1.25m	4ft $1\frac{1}{5}$in
1.5m	4ft 11in
1.75m	5ft $8\frac{9}{10}$in
2m	6ft $6\frac{3}{4}$in
2.25m	7ft $4\frac{3}{5}$in
2.5m	8ft $2\frac{2}{5}$in
3m	9ft $10\frac{1}{10}$in